Before Grenfell

'Shane Ewen's book *Before Grenfell* contains irreplaceable historical context for understanding the causes of the Grenfell Tower fire. The book skewers the mistakes made by ministers and their advisors, who were supposed to set the rules to make our homes safe, but instead gave private profiteers a free hand. It is a well-researched and highly readable account of fire safety and deregulation over the last century. I strongly recommend the book to everyone serious about justice for Grenfell.'

— **Matt Wrack, General Secretary, The Fire Brigades Union, UK**

'In following the threads of this story further back than anyone else, Ewen has produced a compelling, vital and shocking record of the long history which led us to Grenfell Tower.

His masterful work brings to light long forgotten stories and provides an urgent warning about what the future may hold. It is a crucial, urgent contribution to the current debate on fire safety, but also an excoriating story about our shared history and the long running failure of the British state to protect its most vulnerable citizens from fire. It should be read by anyone who cares about this story and many more yet to learn about it.'

— **Peter Apps, Deputy Editor of Inside Housing and author of Show Me The Bodies: How We Let Grenfell Happen.**

'This is a high quality, painstakingly researched and factually accurate piece of scholarship. It has a clear historical approach that convincingly details the relevant trajectory of regulation and deregulation – and a whole lot more – that underpins the Grenfell disaster. I learned a lot from reading it. It will be a go-to guide to relevant legislation, received wisdom and debates about fire safety, science, building standards and regulation'.

— **Stuart Hodkinson, Associate Professor in Critical Urban Geography, University of Leeds, UK.**

'Before Grenfell is a critical contribution to helping us understand why 72 were killed in a fire in the richest borough in London. Ewen's book reveals the decades-long practices that culminated so tragically on the 14th June 2017'.

— **Gill Kernick, Author of Catastrophe and Systemic Change: Learning from the Grenfell Tower Fire and Other Disasters.**

'It is a great and much-needed piece of work that I learnt so much from. In a general sense, it provides an important context for developments (or lack of) that I was aware of but did not fully understand the rationale for. More specifically, it also helps to explain why our human behaviour in dwelling fires research met with indifference from national bodies insofar as they reflected government policy prioritising commercial interests over public safety'.

— **David Wales, Human Experience and Service Design Consultant and Research Manager for 'Human Behaviour in Dwelling Fires' study (2009–16).**

Before Grenfell

Fire, Safety and Deregulation in Twentieth-Century Britain

Shane Ewen

LONDON
INSTITUTE OF HISTORICAL RESEARCH
UNIVERSITY OF LONDON PRESS

Available to purchase in print or download for free at
https://www.sas.ac.uk/publications/grenfell

First published 2023 by
University of London Press
Senate House, Malet St, London WC1E 7HU

A CIP catalogue record for this book is available from The British Library.

ISBNs
978-1-914477-25-6 (hardback)
978-1-914477-26-3 (.pdf)
978-1-914477-28-7 (.epub)

DOI
10.14296/rkft3410

Cover design for University of London Press by Nicky Borowiec.
Text set by Westchester Publishing Services in Adobe Garamond Pro Regular.

Contents

Acknowledgements

I would not have considered writing this book without the initial encouragement of Simon Szreter and Philip Carter and the History & Policy network. I am very grateful to both for early conversations about the proposal, which has inevitably evolved a great deal following the revelations of Sir Martin Moore-Bick's public inquiry and the challenges posed by the Covid-19 pandemic and lockdowns of 2020–1. Emma Gallon has been incredibly supportive as the book has taken form and patiently waited for me to submit the manuscript. Given that the content discussed here should be as widely and freely accessible as possible, I am thankful to the University of London Press for its full support in publishing this in open-access format and I will not be drawing any royalties from its publication. To the two readers who gave constructive feedback on the draft manuscript, thank you so much for your time in helping to shape the final manuscript.

A significant portion of the research and writing process was funded by an Arts and Humanities Research Council Standard Open Grant (AH/N00664X/1), 'Forged by Fire: Burns Injury and Identity in Britain, c.1800–2000'. I am grateful to members of the burns team, Jonathan Reinarz, Rebecca Wynter and Aaron Andrews, for their friendship and intellectual encouragement throughout the evolution of the book. They read draft chapters and gave constructive advice on some of the more challenging aspects of the manuscript, often through virtual coffee breaks. This book contains much of their own emotional labour for which I will always be in their debt. Likewise, members of the project team's steering committee provided help and assistance whenever asked. I also thank History colleagues and students at Leeds Beckett University for their encouragement during recent years, especially as I wrestled with emotionally challenging chapters.

Draft chapters and semi-structured thoughts were presented at several events: the Festival of Ideas, a History & Policy – Home Office seminar and the Bartlett School of Construction's Grenfell Tower seminar series. I am grateful to the organisers of these events and attendees who offered feedback and encouragement. Thanks also to Paul Hampton, Peter Holland, Ronnie King, Chris Smith, Jim Smith, Dave Walton, Matt Wrack and many others in the Fire and Rescue Service, past and present, who have given encouragement along the way. Although there are too many archivists and librarians to name, all of whom have helped with facilitating access to their collections, I'd like to record my gratitude to the fabulous reading room staff at the British Library's Boston Spa site for going above and beyond over the past few years. On a personal level, I am grateful to Sarah and Jarvis for keeping my feet firmly on the ground while working on the project; I could not have finished this book without their emotional support and patience.

I am also indebted to the many safety campaigners I have corresponded with over the years, including the late Sam Webb of Tower Blocks UK. Meeting with Caroline and Siân in 2019 inspired me to persevere with the book through several dark episodes. While this has been a challenging book to write, I trust that it explains the longer-term historical context behind the disaster at Grenfell Tower in 2017 and contributes to the ongoing campaign for justice, security and safety by the local community and others invested in improving standards nationally. Finally, this book is dedicated to all the people who lost their lives in the multiple fires covered in the following pages. Many of the deceased have been long forgotten, but they forever remain in our hearts. To their families and survivors, to the campaigners, activists, trade unionists and others who dedicate their lives to improving public safety, and to the millions of ordinary people currently living in unsafe homes, never give up hope, and never stop fighting for lasting change. Grenfell changed everything; Grenfell changed history.

Introduction

Multiple-fatality fires, deregulation and the value of 'thinking with history'

Families were evacuated and others trapped in smoke-filled flats when fire broke out on the eighth floor of a 20 storey Notting Hill tower block. Now, Grenfell Tower on the Lancaster West Estate has been labelled a 'death trap' by a local ward councillor ... 'People couldn't get out of the place because the design is so bad ... People could have died last night and I lay the blame at the feet of the designer of the building. This place is a death trap'.[1]

This report of a fire without serious casualties at Grenfell Tower in June 1979 assumes an entirely new and frightening meaning in the context of the tragic events of 14 June 2017, when a horrific cladding fire at the same tower caused the deaths of seventy-two people. Tucked into a folder of newspaper cuttings in the archives of the Royal Borough of Kensington and Chelsea (RBKC), the article flags up significant issues for our understanding of the Grenfell disaster: the need for good design, building control and management of higher-risk residential buildings (HRRBs); the responsibility of politicians, architects and emergency services to protect communities vulnerable to fire; and the urgency of improving communication between housing providers, emergency services and residents. In this instance alone, one resident reported being told by a firefighter to 'Get your children and get out down the fire escape', while another was told to stay in her smoke-filled flat with her children: 'I went back in and put wet towels against the door and just prayed.' Another resident reported that a police officer threatened to arrest him if he attempted to enter the building to reach his family.[2]

The RBKC had received criticism for its 'indifference' towards the safety and welfare of its residents during the initial planning consultation on the estate in the 1960s, and there is little evidence to suggest that this attitude had significantly altered following its completion a decade later.[3] Indeed, the RBKC's archives record multiple problems with the

---

[1] Royal Borough of Kensington and Chelsea Archives (hereafter RBKCA), 'Arrest Threat as Families Flee "Death Trap" Blaze', *West London Observer*, 28 June 1979.

[2] RBKCA, 'Arrest Threat'.

[3] RBKCA, Acc/2001/002/Box 14, Kensington Society Conference on Town Planning & Housing in North Kensington, 9 October 1965, 8.

estate's design and management from the mid-1970s to the 2010s – these include anti-social behaviour, structural defects including asbestos and damp, and poor cleanliness, which led to the arrival of unwelcome guests such as cockroaches and rodents – all reported by residents upset by the conditions in which they were expected to live. As one resident angrily complained in a letter to the local paper, 'If only the Kensington and Chelsea Tory Councillors could live on this estate as they seem to think it is so brilliant. They would not spend one night here.'[4] These problems – not least the complaint that the council did not listen to residents' legitimate concerns about living in multi-storey estates – resonate with the findings of historians writing about lived experiences elsewhere in the country.[5] They are similarly echoed by recent studies of the institutional neglect faced by Grenfell Tower's residents when raising safety issues concerned with the building's refurbishment in the years preceding the 2017 fire.[6]

Although the RBKC's official archives record few complaints about fire precautions, we know from published and unpublished collections, including oral testimony, that residents' concerns about structural safety were widespread by the 1990s.[7] The archives collected by local and national stakeholder organisations, including charities, trade unions, fire and rescue services, and other professional associations, have proven useful in providing a more comprehensive and longer-term picture of the problem, drawing upon the perspectives of residents and other building users, architects and fire engineers, and housing and safety campaigners, as well as fire prevention

[4] RBKCA, *Kensington News & Post*, 13 May 1977.

[5] Barry Hazley, Lynn Abrams, Ade Kearns and Valerie Wright, 'Place, Memory and the British High Rise Experience: Negotiating Social Change on the Wyndford Estate, 1962–2015', *Contemporary British History* 35, no. 1 (2021): 72–99; Lynsey Hanley, *Estates: An Intimate History* (London: Granta Books, 2012); John Boughton, *Municipal Dreams: The Rise and Fall of Council Housing* (London: Verso, 2019).

[6] See, eg, Stuart Hodkinson, *Safe as Houses: Private Greed, Political Negligence and Housing Policy after Grenfell* (Manchester: Manchester University Press, 2019); Dan Bulley, Jenny Edkins and Nadine El-Enany, eds., *After Grenfell: Violence, Resistance and Response* (London: Pluto Press, 2019); John Preston, *Grenfell Tower: Preparedness, Race and Disaster Capitalism* (Basingstoke: Palgrave, 2019); Gill Kernick, *Catastrophe and Systemic Change: Learning from the Grenfell Tower Fire and Other Disasters* (London: London Publishing Partnership, 2021); Lucy Easthope, *When the Dust Settles: Stories of Love, Loss and Hope from an Expert in Disaster* (London: Hodder & Stoughton, 2022); Peter Apps, *Show Me the Bodies: How We Let Grenfell Happen* (London: Oneworld Publications, 2022).

[7] See, eg, collections held by the Newham Borough Archives (hereafter NBA). I am grateful to James King, Project Officer at Eastside Community Heritage (hereafter ESCH), for sharing transcripts of interviews he conducted with residents and activists regarding the Ronan Point explosion.

officers and frontline firefighters. Thus, in 1990, a spot survey of five local authorities in England by Sam Webb, the architectural adviser to the National Tower Blocks Network, revealed a catalogue of structural defects concerning the blocks' resistance to fire and means of escape. Webb called for certification of tower blocks to protect residents by subjecting blocks to regular inspection by the local fire brigade and requiring landlords to comply with their instructions, although this was not seriously entertained by central government.[8] We also know that local tenants' associations, including Lancaster West's, issued warnings to residents as far back as the 1970s not to tamper with malfunctioning storage heaters without first seeking expert advice, while several local authorities regularly exhibited fire safety advice to vulnerable communities (women, the elderly and the working classes more generally) from at least the late 1950s once flatted estates and houses in multiple occupancy (HMOs) became more prevalent across the British urban landscape.[9] Such advice was to prevent injury to children and other vulnerable groups, as well as to reduce the risk of fire occurring, which indicates a heightened awareness among residents of what Lynn Abrams et al. call the 'micro-politics of residential space' – safety was the collective responsibility of everyone but it often fell to residents to offer neighbourly advice or, as we shall see, act collectively rather than wait for the council or private landlord to intervene.[10]

Grenfell Tower was developed in the wake of an earlier building disaster at the recently completed twenty-two-storey Ronan Point tower block in the East London borough of Newham in 1968. An explosion involving a gas cooker in a flat on the southeastern corner of the eighteenth floor at 5:45am on 16 May blew out the kitchen and living-room walls, seriously injuring its resident, Ivy Hodge. The explosion led to the progressive collapse of the floors above and below Hodge's flat, killing four residents and injuring seventeen more as living rooms collapsed on top of one another in a vertical domino effect. A fifth resident later died in hospital from her injuries. As one of many high-rise pre-cast concrete heavy-panel system-style blocks built

---

[8] Sam Webb, *Annual Spot Safety Survey* (London: National Tower Blocks Network, 1990). The Network's archives were deposited with the Bishopsgate Institute in 2022. I am extremely grateful to Sam Webb for corresponding with me during the research for this book.

[9] Alistair Cartwright, 'The Un-Ideal Home: Fire Safety, Visual Culture and the LCC (1958–63)', *The London Journal* 46, no. 1 (2021): 66–91.

[10] Lynn Abrams, Ade Kearns, Barry Hazley and Valerie Wright, *Glasgow: High-Rise Homes, Estates and Communities in the Post-War Period* (London: Taylor & Francis, 2020), 98; RBKCA Acc/2001/003/Box 24, 'Newssheet of the Lancaster West Tenants' Association', no. 2 (1976), 5.

by the construction firm Taylor Woodrow-Anglian under licence from the Danish firm Larsen-Nielsen, Ronan Point brought Newham residents' concerns about HRRBs into sharp focus. The subsequent media attention and public inquiry, which have been expertly examined by Holly Smith in her 2020 thesis, revealed a litany of problems relating to structural building safety across the country. These findings prompted a national programme of strengthening industrialised system-built tower blocks as well as government-funded research into progressive collapse.[11] The Ronan Point explosion directly led to improvements to England and Wales's Building Regulations in order to protect against extreme shocks to a building such as gas explosion or fire. Introduced in the early 1970s, these regulations, more prescriptive than those in place since the mid-1980s, formed the basis for the subsequent development of Grenfell Tower, which explains why the structure did not collapse under the intense heat in 2017 (indeed, the Lancaster West estate's architect stated a year before the fire that the tower 'could last another 100 years'[12]).

The cause of the 2017 fire is the focus of an extant public inquiry and an ongoing police investigation, and is not the subject of this book. The inquiry, headed by Sir Martin Moore-Bick, a retired judge, was announced by the prime minister, Theresa May, the day after the fire. Formally convened in August 2017 following tense public meetings between Moore-Bick and the local community, representatives of whom were justly demanding greater transparency to the formal proceedings, hearings started in May 2018 and drew to a close in November 2022, with the final report scheduled to appear in 2023.[13] It has been ascertained, as per the Phase One report, that the tower had been disastrously refurbished from 2012–16: the over-cladding of the building with a new insulation and rainscreen cladding system effectively added a new highly combustible external wall to the tower composed of outer aluminium composite material (ACM) rainscreen panels with plastic (polyethylene) cores and foam insulation boards behind.[14] It had earlier been revealed in documents leaked to the media that a more expensive

---

[11] Holly Smith, 'The Ronan Point Scandal, 1968–1993', University of Cambridge MPhil, 2020. The inquiry papers and other documents are held by London Metropolitan Archives (hereafter LMA) GLC/AR/ENG/SE/1/1-9.

[12] Quoted in Hodkinson, *Safe*, 2; ESCH 2018_esch_RoPo_04, Interview with Sam Webb, 20 March 2019.

[13] The proceedings of the inquiry are available at <https://www.grenfelltowerinquiry.org.uk>.

[14] The refurbishment programme is detailed in Martin Moore-Bick, *Grenfell Tower Inquiry: Phase 1 Report – Volume 1* (London: HMSO, 2019), 33–51.

non-combustible cladding, comprising zinc panels with a mineral-rich fire-retardant core, was replaced with the cheaper but flammable alternative, resulting in savings to the RBKC's refurbishment budget of almost £300,000.[15]

Originating in a faulty fridge-freezer in a fourth-floor flat, the fire ignited the external cladding system and spread up the east face of the tower within fifteen minutes. The twenty-four-storey block was enveloped in a frightening sheet of flame, with horrific images screened live on rolling twenty-four-hour news channels and social media. Almost half the number of residents present in the tower opted not to follow the official 'stay put' advice, choosing to self-evacuate the building in the first forty-five minutes of the fire. Of those who remained in the tower, London Fire Brigade estimated that around sixty-five residents were rescued by firefighters once the 'stay put' advice had been revoked in the early hours of the morning. This followed the failure of the building's passive defences, resulting in fire and smoke penetrating the tower, entering flats and spreading internally. Subsequent government-funded tests found that the cladding materials, which were supposed to provide forty minutes' resistance to fire in order to allow firefighters to access the building and, if necessary, evacuate it, failed within nine minutes of ignition, therefore indicating that the external walls of the building failed to comply with building regulations. In all, it took the combined efforts of 250 firefighters and 70 fire engines roughly 60 hours to extinguish the fire and rescue trapped residents.[16]

As its title indicates, *Before Grenfell: Fire, Safety and Deregulation in Twentieth-Century Britain* is not chiefly concerned with the causes of the Grenfell 'atrocity', as it has been described.[17] It is instead focused on the historical circumstances that created the conditions under which the fire occurred. Inevitably this has involved tracing the evolution and subsequent recasting of Britain's building regulations and its national system of fire precautions, both of which were developed incrementally over the twentieth century (and indeed earlier still). Moreover, this book will draw parallels between historic cases of failure and evidence presented to the public inquiry, delving further into history than other recent publications, and taking a wider net to the high number of largely forgotten multiple-fatality fires that

---

[15] *The Guardian*, 30 June 2017, <https://www.theguardian.com/uk-news/2017/jun/30/grenfell-cladding-was-changed-to-cheaper-version-reports-say>.

[16] Martin Moore-Bick, *Grenfell Tower Inquiry: Phase 1 Report Overview* (2019), 4–6, 18–19, 23–4; *BBC News*, 29 October 2019, <https://www.bbc.co.uk/news/uk-40301289>.

[17] Bulley, Edkins and El-Enany, *After Grenfell*, xii.

have occurred in Britain and further afield across the twentieth century, but especially since the end of the Second World War.[18]

The Grenfell fire, we shall see, was less a bolt from the blue than the outcome of an accumulation of decisions and non-decisions, as well as systemic failures at the heart of government to learn from past multiple-fatality fires. It was a fire that was more than forty years in the making, the result of a dangerously casual approach towards construction standards and safety. As academics working within the multi-disciplinary field of disaster studies – which includes environmental and urban historians as well as social historians of technology – have shown, disasters unravel slowly over time due to erroneous assumptions, misinformation and misunderstandings within responsible organisations, as well as failures of governance and regulation, the consequences of which take time to percolate. The cumulative effect of decisions taken for economic, social and political reasons, disasters sometimes take decades to occur, unravelling 'gradually and out of sight' before exploding in dramatic and tragic fashion.[19] Brenna Bhandar has argued that the fire was the culmination of a decades-long 'organised abandonment' by the state in its provision of 'basic levels of safety and security' to all its citizens and it is difficult to dispute this conclusion.[20]

State abandonment is most evident in criticisms of Britain's building regulations and central government's unwillingness to reintroduce tougher codes designed to protect public safety. Within the first year following the Grenfell fire, a succession of investigations by journalists and building safety experts, as well as an Independent Review of Building Regulations and Fire Safety headed by Dame Judith Hackitt, a former chair of the Health and Safety Executive, identified systemic faults in the oversight of building safety but failed to assess the regulations themselves or how they

---

[18] See, eg, Peter Apps cites the Ronan Point explosion and the 1973 fire at Summerland Leisure Centre on the Isle of Man as historic precursors of the 2017 fire (Apps, *Show Me the Bodies*, 28–31), while Gill Kernick cites additional fires at Knowsley Heights, Liverpool (1991), Garnock Court, Irvine (1999), Harrow Court, Stevenage (2005) and Lakanal House, London (2009): Kernick, *Catastrophe*, 29–30.

[19] Rob Nixon, *Slow Violence and the Environmentalism of the Poor* (Cambridge, MA: Harvard University Press, 2011), 2; Scott Gabriel Knowles, 'Learning from Disaster? The History of Technology and the Future of Disaster Research', *Technology and Culture* 55, no. 4 (2014): 773–84; Shane Ewen, 'Socio-Technological Disasters and Engineering Expertise in Victorian Britain: The Holmfirth and Sheffield Floods of 1852 and 1864', *Journal of Historical Geography* 46 (2014): 13–25.

[20] Brenna Bhandar, 'Organised State Abandonment: The Meaning of Grenfell', *The Sociological Review Blog*, 19 September 2018, <https://criticallegalthinking.com/2018/09/21/organised-state-abandonment-the-meaning-of-grenfell>.

were multifariously interpreted by construction industry professionals.[21] Less still has been written about the evolution of building regulations over time and how they were often reformed following major building failures; Hackitt's interim report, published six months after the fire, contains a short historical chapter but little analysis of the political, economic and cultural factors that shaped the present deregulated system.[22]

A few studies have delved deeper into the underlying issues, revealing the complex web of decisions, loopholes and failures that have created what journalist Peter Apps calls 'a national crisis which continues to grip the country today'.[23] In early 2018, writing for *Inside Housing* magazine, Apps and colleagues published a forensic review of regulatory failures dating back to the early 1990s, which subsequently formed the basis for his excellent recent book which hopefully takes the 'national scandal' to a wider readership. Meanwhile, Andrew O'Hagan cited 'a concatenation of failures at the level of industry regulation and building controls' in his 2018 feature article for the *London Review of Books*, albeit with only fleeting references to the historical context.[24] For academics working in the specialist fields of engineering and the built environment, many of the issues facing HRRBs over-clad in combustible materials presented several 'obvious problems' to public safety, but these only really become obvious to the lay reader when placed in their full historic circumstances: materials deemed to satisfy regulations which ignited easily; the rapid spread of fire vertically, laterally and through the building, indicating a lack of fire-breaks and effective compartmentation; and the fire being difficult to extinguish.[25]

A deregulated system of building control was actively fostered by industry and government actors, often working in tandem. The records of government – both the published accounts of Hansard, available in UK Parliamentary Papers, and the unpublished correspondence, memoranda and minutes of

[21] Judith Hackitt, *Building a Safer Future: Independent Review of Building Regulations and Fire Safety – Final Report*, Cmd. 9607 (London: HMSO, 2018).

[22] Judith Hackitt, *Building a Safer Future: Independent Review of Building Regulations and Fire Safety – Interim Report*, Cmd. 9951 (London: HMSO, 2017), 30–5.

[23] Apps, *Show Me the Bodies*, 281.

[24] Peter Apps, Luke Barratt and Sophie Barnes, 'The Paper Trail: The Failure of Building Regulations', *Inside Housing*, 23 March 2018, <https://www.insidehousing.co.uk/news/news/the-paper-trail-the-failure-of-building-regulations-55445>; Andrew O'Hagan, 'The Tower', *London Review of Books*, 7 June 2018, <https://www.lrb.co.uk/v40/n11/andrew-ohagan/the-tower>.

[25] Christopher Gorse and John Sturges, 'Not What Anyone Wanted: Observations on Regulations, Standards, Quality and Experience in the Wake of Grenfell', *Construction Research and Innovation* 8, no. 3 (2017): 72.

relevant departments which have been consulted in the National Archives – indicate growing support for deregulating building control at the heart of government from the start of the 1980s. Over time, central government withdrew from its historic role in maintaining minimum standards of public health and safety (being careful not to admit such on public record), leaving the object of regulation – the building and construction products industries – to become the main vehicle for regulating their own products and practices. *Before Grenfell* traces this cultural change in the operation of government and its regulation of building control and fire safety across the twentieth century. Only with a fuller historical approach can we expect to reasonably understand *how* the Grenfell fire was allowed to happen. In Chapter 1 I argue that a longer-term picture of the evolution of building rules in England and Wales – shifting from a discretionary system of model byelaws introduced in the second half of the nineteenth century to prescriptive national regulations by the mid-1960s, which were later 'recast' as functional regulations two decades later – is important in explaining the 'bewildering and sometimes apparently contradictory directions provided by building regulations' in operation by the twenty-first century, creating a culture of competition and self-regulation that so disastrously culminated in the 2017 fire.[26]

In addition to the deregulation of building control and abandonment of effective enforcement measures, commentators have cited a raft of evidence to illustrate the 'benign neglect' of fire safety since at least the turn of the twenty-first century. Whereas once fire precautions were subject to inspection and enforcement by experienced firefighters in a number of sectors, this was no longer the case following major reforms to the fire and rescue service. Alongside this, responsibility for risk assessment and mitigation was outsourced to individuals – the designated 'responsible person' – in the 2000s, who could be someone with the minimum level of training rather than a public servant experienced in the prevention of fires. Many of the proposals to reduce the powers of inspection, certification and enforcement by fire brigades, and to introduce greater individual responsibility for safety, originated in the 1980s and 1990s and were often expressed in terms of the necessity to reduce 'burdens on business' by freeing the individual from the bureaucracy of inspections and form-filling. These criticisms of fire precautions, which were first introduced in the early 1970s to strengthen the standard of safety in a number of sectors (particularly the hotel and boarding-house industry), and their subsequent curtailment and dismantling, form the focus of Chapter 2. The justifications for the swingeing

---

[26] Gorse and Sturge, 'Not What Anyone Wanted', 72.

cuts to the funding and resourcing of the fire and rescue service in the five years leading up to 2015 – these included reducing the numbers of both fire prevention staff and safety inspections – are traceable to the New Labour Government's fire service reform agenda of the early 2000s, as well as being a major consequence of the 'austerity' programme introduced by the Conservative-Liberal Democrat Coalition Government in 2010. Although safety regulations have, as we shall see, demonstrably saved lives, they have regularly been cited as examples of 'red tape' that interfere with personal freedoms and stymie economic growth by successive governments.[27]

This book is a history of deregulation that situates the horrific events of 14 June 2017 in their longer-term political and social context. As Knud Andresen and Stefan Müller explain, support for deregulation emerged during the 1970s from critics who saw the state as being 'too powerful' over the everyday routines of social and economic life. In particular, there was a strongly held belief that free markets were being strangled by state intervention and what was needed was far-ranging deregulation rather than more controls. This led to a concerted push – from outside government, for instance from business and the popular media, but also increasingly from within – to 'loosen its grasp and remodel it from an interventional and regulatory state into a merely controlling state'.[28] Deregulation, then, is as much an ideological change in how powerful political and economic forces view the role of the state in governing society and the economy as it is a set of working practices designed to restrict the state's regulatory control over everyday life. For the purposes of this book, deregulation refers to a coordinated series of policies and practices that seek to relax or remove existing regulatory controls over the private sector and leave the market responsible for its own regulation; that is, the object of regulation becomes the *de facto* regulator of itself. Deregulation also involved shifting from a prescriptive to a more discretionary set of controls, as well as devolving greater responsibility for safety onto the individual (that is, through

[27] Sian Moore, Tessa Wright and Philip Taylor, *Fighting Fire: One Hundred Years of the Fire Brigades Union* (Oxford: New Internationalist, 2018), 44–5; Tony Prosser and Mark Taylor, *The Grenfell Tower Fire: Benign Neglect and the Road to an Avoidable Tragedy* (Shoreham-by-Sea: Pavilion Publishing, 2020); Fire Brigades Union, *The Grenfell Tower Fire: A Fire Caused by Profit and Deregulation* (Kingston upon Thames: Fire Brigades Union, 2019).
[28] Knud Andresen and Stefan Müller, 'Contesting Deregulation: The 1970s as a Turning Point in Western History? Introductory Remarks', in Andresen and Müller, eds., *Contesting Deregulation: Debates, Practices and Developments in the West since the 1970s* (New York: Berghahn Books, 2017), 4; Adrian Williamson, *Conservative Economic Policymaking and the Birth of Thatcherism, 1964–1979* (New York: Palgrave, 2015), 24.

self-regulation or, in certain key instances, self-compliance measures). This is based on the understanding, entrenched within neoliberal thinking since the late 1970s, that the duty holder is better placed to know their obligations to the safety of those for whom they are responsible rather than waiting for the state to tell them what to do and how to do it.[29]

Deregulation was part of a series of methods used by neoliberal governments from the late 1970s through to the 2010s to weaken the public sector and reduce the state's control over everyday life in preference for empowering the free market to regulate its own affairs. These included, as we shall see in Chapter 3, the privatisation of public services, including building and fire safety research. For a large part of the post-war period, the responsibility for providing the infrastructure and funding for scientific research into fire safety rested jointly with the state and the insurance industry, with public safety accepted as the core priority of the work undertaken by the Building Research Establishment (BRE) and its predecessors. After its sale in 1997, however, BRE lost sight of its historic public safety role, becoming a highly competitive organisation geared towards fulfilling its contractual obligations to its customers, many of whom came from the building and construction products industries. The privatisation of fire research deprioritised the significance of public safety by adopting the dubious maxim that commercial testing information was confidential. It is interesting to note that a few lone voices – notably following a motion passed at the Fire Brigades Union's annual conference in 2022[30] – have called for BRE's return to public ownership in the wake of the Grenfell fire.

Historians of twentieth-century Britain have increasingly turned their focus to the changing relationship between the state and its social obligations since the 1980s and, in some instances, earlier. Between them, Hilary Cooper and Simon Szreter, Paul Almond and Mike Esbester, and Christopher Sirrs have described a multitude of policies – including monetarism, privatisation and the growing use of 'light-touch' discretionary powers – as marking a decisive shift from a relatively narrow conception of mid-twentieth-century governance that centred on employers, organised labour and regulators to a larger, more diffuse coalition of corporate and financial interests, third-sector organisations and individuals at the turn

---

[29] Robert M. Ledger, '"A Transition from Here to There?" Neo-Liberal Thought and Thatcherism', Queen Mary University PhD thesis, 2014.

[30] Fire Brigades Union, 'FBU Calls for Grenfell Building Safety Body to Be Nationalised', 13 May 2022, <https://www.fbu.org.uk/news/2022/05/13/fbu-calls-grenfell-building-safety-body-be-nationalised>.

of the present century.[31] At its core, deregulation has served as a loosely coordinated set of policies by which successive governments since the 1970s have governed. Notwithstanding the political differences between governments, the broad outcome has seen the emergence of a 'neoliberal age' in which the values and interests of free trade economics and private financial institutions are given priority as the main determinants of progress in society, as a recent edited collection has charted.[32] This has been at the expense of what Sam Wetherell calls the 'developmental and social aims' that guided mid-twentieth-century Conservative and Labour governments in building a socially progressive and more equal society through the visible hand of the state.[33]

British economic and political historians have most closely aligned deregulation with the 'Big Bang' of the mid-1980s, which involved a reduction in state controls over the governance of banks and other financial institutions, chiefly as a means to boost the competitiveness of British financial services with competitors overseas.[34] The economist's traditional view of regulation, that it adds unwelcome costs to business, has held sway across much of the literature: 'Competition when possible, regulation where necessary.'[35] However, historians have also started to examine the evolution of ideas and practices related to deregulation as they pertain to other areas of government work beyond financial institutions, including

[31] Hilary Cooper and Simon Szreter, *After the Virus: Lessons from the Past for a Better Future* (Cambridge: Cambridge University Press, 2021), 70–1; Paul Almond and Mike Esbester, 'Legitimate Risks? Occupational Health and Safety and the Public in Britain, c. 1960–2015', in Tom Crook and Mike Esbester, eds., *Governing Risks in Modern Britain: Danger, Safety and Accidents c. 1800–2000* (London: Palgrave Macmillan, 2016), 280; Christopher Sirrs, 'Health and Safety in the British Regulatory State, 1961–2001: The HSC, HSE and the Management of Occupational Risk', London School of Hygiene & Tropical Medicine PhD thesis, 2016, 276–9.

[32] Aled Davies, Ben Jackson and Florence Sutcliffe-Braithwaite, eds., *The Neoliberal Age? Britain since the 1970s* (London: University College London Press, 2021).

[33] Sam Wetherell, *Foundations: How the Built Environment Made Twentieth-Century Britain* (Princeton, NJ: Princeton University Press, 2020), 11–12.

[34] Aled Davies, 'The Roots of Britain's Financialised Political Economy', in Davies, Jackson and Sutcliffe-Braithwaite, *Neoliberal Age*, 299–318; Robert M. Ledger, *Power and Political Economy from Thatcher to Blair: The Great Enemy of Democracy?* (London: Routledge, 2021); Forrest Capie, 'Financial Deregulation in the United Kingdom', in Alexis Drach and Youssef Cassis, eds., *Financial Deregulation: A Historical Perspective* (Oxford: Oxford University Press, 2021), 48.

[35] John Kay and John Vickers, 'Regulatory Reform in Britain', *Economic Policy* 3, no. 7 (1988): 287.

urban regeneration and the allocation of enterprise zones.[36] Similar tactics were used in housing policy to incrementally deregulate the private rental market in the late 1980s[37] and, as we shall see, in building regulations and fire precautions at various stages between the 1980s and 2000s. Research into deregulation has also extended into the realm of home, parenthood and family life where government policies have impacted upon interpersonal relationships and the work–life balance. For example, Florence Sutcliffe-Braithwaite has traced how this new way of thinking was used to unravel the post-war system of state-led, paternalistic welfare provision in preference for a family-centred, moralistic individualism with the ascendancy of Thatcherism from the late 1970s, which has been echoed by Helen McCarthy in her study of working women and motherhood.[38]

Deregulation was a preferred strategy for governments of different political shades, proliferating on the world stage as a central tool of the ascendancy of the neoliberal world order during the final decades of the twentieth century.[39] Deregulation was similarly used to remove or rescind safety laws in American business during the 1970s and 1980s, reflecting a 'more callous and divided' nation where government 'had essentially given up on protecting its most vulnerable and precarious citizens'.[40] Nor did deregulation emerge in Britain with the election of the Thatcher Government in 1979, important though that moment undoubtedly was in heralding the acceleration of the 'market-driven politics' of the 1980s and 1990s.[41] For instance, James Vernon has shown how both Conservative and Labour governments of the 1960s and 1970s introduced forms of economic liberalisation such as the deregulation and outsourcing of security two decades before Heathrow

[36] Ledger, 'A Transition from Here to There?', 107; Sam Wetherell, 'Freedom Planned: Enterprise Zones and Urban Non-Planning in Post-War Britain', *Twentieth-Century British History* 27, no. 2 (2016): 266–89.

[37] Jim Tomlinson, 'The Failures of Neoliberalism in Britain since the 1970s: The Limits on "Market Forces" in a Deindustrialising Economy and a "New Speenhamland"', in Davies, Jackson and Sutcliffe-Braithwaite, *Neoliberal Age*, 99.

[38] Florence Sutcliffe-Braithwaite, 'Neo-Liberalism and Morality in the Making of Thatcherite Social Policy', *Historical Journal* 55, no. 2 (2012): 497–520; Helen McCarthy, '"I Don't Know How She Does It!" Feminism, Family and Work in "Neoliberal" Britain', in Davies, Jackson and Sutcliffe-Braithwaite, *Neoliberal Age*, 135–54.

[39] Gary Gerstle, *The Rise and Fall of the Neoliberal Order: America and the World in the Free Market Era* (Oxford: Oxford University Press, 2022).

[40] Bryant Simon, *The Hamlet Fire: A Tragic Story of Cheap Food, Cheap Government, and Cheap Lives* (New York: The New Press, 2017), 15.

[41] Colin Leys, *Market-Driven Politics: Neoliberal Democracy and the Public Interest* (London: Verso, 2001).

Airport was privatised in 1986.[42] Likewise, moves towards a deregulated fire safety sector can be traced from the privatisation of routine research and testing in the early 1970s. Nevertheless, these examples collectively illustrate a desire by the modern neoliberal state to free the economy from controls, dismantle the model of state-orientated welfare capitalism and establish a stronger connection between individual responsibility and freedom. As Stephen Brooke has argued, deregulation helped speed up the scale and pace of change to everyday life in late twentieth-century Britain and facilitate access to an increasingly globalised marketplace of ideas, capital and people.[43]

Paradoxically, deregulation has never meant an end to all regulation and has occasionally involved the creation of new or additional regulations, as several authors have shown. It has also necessitated a greater use of internal checks and inspections by professional bodies as well as individual firms as part of the growing trend towards self-regulation, which was embraced by government ministers during the 1980s and 1990s.[44] But, as Michael Moran has shown, self-regulation is itself a 'hard-to-clarify' concept because it has evolved incrementally as a largely undefined 'regulatory ideology' that has in practice been 'mobilized to legitimize any number of particular institutional arrangements'. Self-regulatory systems have therefore developed as a form of 'quasi-government' with tools ranging from 'entirely informal sets of practices to those that, involving more direct control of regulatory systems by central government, shade off into systems of state control'.[45] This, according to William Davies, requires the state to exert 'an active force' in enabling such ideas and practices to be rolled out; it 'cannot simply rely on "market forces"'.[46] Giandomenico Majone reveals the 1980s as the decade when regulation became 'the new battleground of ideas on industrial and social policy' and, while writers have generally seen Margaret Thatcher's Conservative governments of 1979–90 as presiding over a substantial reduction in controls over public services, it should be noted that

[42] James Vernon, 'Heathrow and the Making of Neoliberal Britain', *Past & Present* 252 (2021): 213–47.

[43] Stephen Brooke, 'Living in "New Times": Historicizing 1980s Britain', *History Compass* 12, no. 1 (2014): 24.

[44] Capie, 'Financial Deregulation', 49.

[45] Michael Moran, *The British Regulatory State: High Modernism and Hyper-Inflation* (Oxford: Oxford University Press, 2007), 67.

[46] William Davies, 'Neoliberalism: A Bibliographic Review', *Theory, Culture & Society* 1, nos. 7–8 (2014): 310.

her governments also extended statutory regulations.[47] This was the case, as we shall see, with fire precautions, in which successive governments took a path of least intervention, either by creating new statutory regulations as discretionary powers or by proceeding on a 'regulate-to-deregulate' basis;[48] that is, in cases where a new regulation was introduced to strengthen the governance of fire safety in notoriously high-risk premises – invariably following multiple-fatality disasters such as those at Bradford City's Valley Parade stadium in 1985 and King's Cross Underground station two years later – this was offset by the relaxation of existing regulations as applied to lower-risk premises. We also see the paradox of deregulation in central government's persistent refusal to introduce licensing of HMOs throughout the 1980s and 1990s on the basis that existing discretionary powers allowed local authorities to effectively regulate the private rental housing sector despite the high number of fatalities in fires in bedsits, lodging houses and hostels. Chapters 2 and 4 will explore the historic connections between the impulse to deregulate and the necessity for governments to be seen to regulate in the interests of public safety as they applied to different 'at-risk' premises, including hotels, care homes and hostels, thereby illustrating how deregulation is itself contested terrain between competing ideas, institutions and extra-institutional actors.

What can a historical approach contribute to our understanding of the Grenfell disaster and 'to ensure another Grenfell never happens again'?[49] First of all, *Before Grenfell* offers a longer-term perspective on issues that did not form an integral part of the inquiry's remit. While Sir Martin Moore-Bick references earlier milestones in building regulation, 'stay put' and multiple-fatality tower-block fires (notably in a section titled 'Before Grenfell' in which he briefly examines the fire at Lakanal House in South London in 2009, which caused the deaths of six residents, including three young children), these are generally only included as background details in his Phase 1 Report.[50] Even then, with a couple of important exceptions, the proceedings and evidence trail tend not to go back much before the present century, which is unsurprising given the skill and patience required in

---

[47] Giandomenico Majone, 'Paradoxes of Privatization and Deregulation', *Journal of European Public Policy* 1, no. 1 (1994): 54; Philip Booth, *Thatcher: The Myth of Deregulation*, IEA Discussion Paper No. 60 (London: Institute of Economic Affairs, 2015).

[48] Ng Sek Hong and Chris Rowley, 'Globalization and Hong Kong's Labour Market: The Deregulation Paradox', *Asia Pacific Business Review* 6, nos. 3–4 (2000): 174–92.

[49] Grenfell United's statement supporting its #DemandCharges campaign, 16 December 2021, <https://grenfellunited.org.uk/latest/demandcharges>.

[50] Moore-Bick, *Phase 1 Report*, 73–5.

piecing together records from an earlier, pre-digital age.[51] By tracing the waves of building regulation, fire precautions and scientific testing of materials over the past century or longer, drawing on the records of several prominent and lesser-known institutions (these include the Joint Fire Research Organisation and its Fire Research Station, the Central Fire Brigades Advisory Council and Fire Brigades Union, and numerous specialist periodicals published across the fire and construction sectors), we are able to situate Grenfell in its historic context and recognise its significance as an unintended but not unanticipated outcome of the state's deregulation of public safety.

Secondly, in *Why History Matters*, John Tosh argues that 'thinking with history' performs a vital role in supporting the function of democratic society by illuminating and deepening current issues. As a way of thinking and a discrete academic discipline, history is also important in demonstrating how the present is both connected to and a product of the past. The historian's role is less to teach specific lessons drawn from the past than to provide the evidence and interpretative framework through which readers can make their own informed judgements about the issues of the day.[52] This applies as much to policymakers, whose principal consideration for decision making is previous policy, as it does to those communities who are directly affected by the decisions taken on their behalf. *Before Grenfell* offers a critical historical account of the evolution of fire safety research and practice across the twentieth century, but with a particular focus on the period between the 1970s and the present century, to deepen the reader's understanding of the complexity of the current issues and their contested perspectives. Following Alix Green's cue expressed in *History, Policy and Public Purpose*, I have sought in this book to write 'history with public purpose', and my argument and approach here has been shaped by two decades of researching, writing and speaking about the British fire and rescue service to a variety of audiences, including civil servants, trade unionists and other stakeholders.[53]

This builds towards, thirdly, plugging what Green calls the 'history gap' that exists in contemporary policymaking. Historians have noted that the British government repeatedly fails to learn from past policy successes and failures because of its lack of institutional memory and its inability to use

---

[51] Those witnesses who took the most historically informed approach to their testimony were Sam Webb, architect and safety campaigner; Matt Wrack, general secretary of the Fire Brigades Union; and Luke Bisby, professor of fire at the University of Edinburgh.

[52] John Tosh, *Why History Matters* (Basingstoke: Palgrave Macmillan, 2008), 120–1.

[53] Alix R. Green, *History, Policy and Public Purpose: Historians and Historical Thinking in Government* (Basingstoke: Palgrave Macmillan, 2016), 42.

history as either a 'way of thinking' or a resource for 'good' policymaking.[54] This is no less evident in the fields of fire service and housing policy, which have been subject to multiple 'machinery of government' changes since the 1990s, leading to a significant hollowing-out of civil servants' skills. Fire and rescue service policy has resided with four different government departments since 1997,[55] while, as of January 2023, there have been twenty-three housing ministers in post over the same period, serving an average term of a little over one year (there were five different ministers or under-secretaries alone in 2022 as the present government lurched from crisis to crisis). These startling, if unsurprising, revelations reflect the low priority given to housing and fire policy by successive governments, as well as the 'benign neglect' of fire safety issues. They also reveal a discontinuity in policymaking, which has caused more harm than good to those who are most vulnerable to injury or death, as monstrously illustrated on 14 June 2017. It is my contention that responsible policies will only emerge following serious engagement with the tools and skills prevalent within the historical discipline; policymaking necessitates learning *with* history as well as learning *from* history. Until that happens, ministers will continue to play with fire and we will all nervously sleep with one eye open.

---

[54] Green, *History, Policy and Public Purpose*, 43, 48; Lucy Delap, Simon Szreter and Fiona Holland, 'History as a Resource for the Future: Building Civil Service Skills', *History & Policy*, 15 July 2014, <https://www.historyandpolicy.org/consultations/consultations/history-as-a-resource-for-the-future-building-civil-service-skills>.

[55] These were the Home Office, Department of Transport and the Regions, Office of the Deputy Prime Minister and the Department for Communities and Local Government, before returning to the stewardship of the Home Office in 2016.

1. From byelaws to building regulations: recasting building control in Britain since the nineteenth century

In a talk to the Royal Society of Arts in March 1945, the Liverpool city surveyor George Pierce Clingan was one of the first construction professionals to publicly foresee the creation of a national code of building regulations:

> That eventually the numerous local planning schemes will be merged into one national scheme seems inevitable; and, as a corollary to this, there should surely be a national code of building regulations. It goes without saying ... that the code should be specifically framed to encourage that natural diversity in both design and materials which springs from individual taste, local traditions and the desire to use local building materials.[1]

The speech aroused interest at a time when bold solutions were being publicised for addressing the severe housing shortages caused by wartime destruction, as well as planning bottlenecks that delayed the process of physical reconstruction. A national code, Clingan conceived, would also act as a check on poor construction by enforcing a uniform standard of control through 'the appointment of thoroughly qualified' and 'wholly independent' surveyors across the whole country.[2]

Clingan, a fellow of the Incorporated Association of Architects and Surveyors (IAAS) and member of the Institute of Structural Engineers, did not speak on behalf of the profession as a whole, however.[3] *The Surveyor and Municipal and County Engineer*, while endorsing his general proposal for national standards, rejected the suggestion that a separate ministry be formed within central government to oversee building. Instead, it proposed the formation of an independent body composed of local authorities, surveyors, architects and building trades organisations who 'should have

---

[1] G.P. Clingan, 'National Building Regulations', *Journal of the Royal Society of Arts* 93, no. 4688 (1945): 207.

[2] Clingan, 'National Building Regulations', 208; *Liverpool Evening Express*, 31 January 1945, 3; *Liverpool Daily Post*, 1 February 1945, 2; *The Times*, 31 January 1945, 5; *The Municipal Journal & Local Government Administrator* (hereafter *MJ*), 16 February 1945, 339.

[3] *Liverpool Evening Express*, 1 September 1943, 2.

some degree of responsibility' for raising the standard of construction across the board.[4]

For others, the scale of the task ahead could only be met with a simplified system of building control – including fewer controls over the use of new materials at a time of shortages in traditional materials (brick, timber and plasterboard especially) and skilled workers. This would free firms from the public constraints imposed upon them to build quickly in order to meet housing demand. Conservative MP Arthur Bossom, himself an architect, asserted that 'any useless and out-of-date regulations should be scrapped. Others should be simplified. All of them should be standardised and full use of the latest and most scientific knowledge should be allowed throughout the country'. Many of the solutions to Britain's building crisis – particularly prefabricated houses and the greater use of steel and concrete – would reduce costs while speeding up construction if only the regulations would permit industry the freedom and flexibility to build.[5]

For Clingan, the solution was not to scrap existing regulations but to strengthen them: 'we appear to have accepted the fact that the old-time individual freedom in building enterprise must cease'. Instead, he and many other professionals advocated codification of building byelaws on a national footing in order to avoid the diversity of practice that existed across the country. In particular, he cited his preference for a national code 'on the lines of the present London regulations', which he considered to produce an improved standard of house compared to those built under the model byelaws that operated in provincial Britain. London had been governed by an advanced system of building regulations since its Great Fire of 1666, whereas a uniform scheme of provincial byelaws, with a greater degree of flexibility than those that operated in London, had only been rolled out from the mid-nineteenth century. Much like what had occurred in seventeenth-century London, where conflagration triggered the modernisation of the capital's built fabric, the levelling of wartime Britain presented an opportunity to rebuild on a national scale. 'Catastrophic devastation has been wrought for us not in five days but during more than five long war-years', said Clingan, 'and not in London only, but throughout the land; and schemes galore – national and local – testify to the fact that building regulations on a national scale are inevitable if the situation is to be saved.'[6]

Clingan's views coincided with two seismic changes in mid-century political thinking: first, the pressing need for greater state planning and

---

[4] *The Surveyor and Municipal and County Engineer*, 9 February 1945, 73–4, 84.
[5] See Alfred Bossom's introduction to Clingan, 'National Building Regulations', 204–5.
[6] Clingan, 'National Building Regulations', 206.

control in order to improve standards of construction; and second, a growing mistrust of local authorities to deliver this without stronger oversight from Whitehall. Only with national standards of construction, uniformly enforced by professionally accredited surveyors, could a socially progressive post-war nation be built. Improved standards would form the foundation for the building of what Sam Wetherell calls a 'developmental social infrastructure' of discrete and recognisable spatial forms ranging from the housing estate to the shopping centre.[7] And although national building regulations were not introduced until the mid-1960s – post-war governments had other priorities in housing and welfare reform – the fact that it was being openly discussed for the first time indicates the emerging consensus that uniform regulations produced good-quality buildings and, consequently, improved the quality of life for tens of millions of British people.

Yet it was Bossom's call for a simplified regulatory system which echoed across the country and reshaped the built environment in the longer term. It is also an anti-regulatory view that resonated strongly with construction industry leaders, senior civil servants and ex-government ministers in their witness testimony to the Grenfell Inquiry, despite simplistic claims by a former senior government minister that the fire 'is not about deregulation'.[8] Building regulations were repeatedly criticised from the late 1960s as 'extremely complex' and 'unwieldy, inflexible, unduly restrictive and confusing' by many in the construction industry.[9] A populist discourse of anti-red-tapeism was recognisable within right-wing newspapers from at least the mid-1970s, coinciding with an ideological shift in the Conservative Party leadership in favour of greater competition and choice in the provision of public services and a diminished role for the state. As a number of historians have shown, this monetarist approach manifested itself most strongly during the 1980s with public expenditure restrictions accompanied by a co-ordinated programme of privatisation and deregulation, selling off state assets while limiting the capacity of state regulation through a curtailment of legislative controls, especially among local authorities. Central government set out to rebuild the built environment according to a set of ideological values that

---

[7] Wetherell, *Foundations*, 3, 7.

[8] Grenfell Tower Inquiry (hereafter GTI), 7 April 2022, Testimony of Lord Pickles, Secretary of State for Communities and Local Government (2010–15), 458.

[9] W.S. Wright and Vincent Powell-Smith, *The Building Regulations Explained and Illustrated for Residential Buildings: A Guide for Students and Others* (London: Crosby Lockwood & Son, 1967), iii; 5th edition, 1978, vii; A.J. Elder, *Guide to the Building Regulations 1985*, 2nd edition (London: Butterworth Architecture, 1986), 2.

prioritised the virtues of the marketplace over its social responsibilities towards its citizens.[10] Building regulations were 'recast' in the mid-1980s, and further revised in the 1990s and 2000s, introducing greater flexibility as well as competition within the compliance framework. The goal of modern neoliberal governments, according to Majone, was to introduce 'less restrictive or rigid regulation, rather than no regulation', which in Britain led to the institutionalisation of 'regulation without enforcement' in a variety of policy areas ranging from environmental and food protections to building safety.[11]

Several historians have traced the prevalence of anti-regulatory interests within government since at least the second half of the nineteenth century. Policymakers preferred to take the path of least intervention, utilising permissive powers at the expense of prescriptive measures wherever possible. Several safety inspectorates were created in the Victorian period, which monitored standards of regulation across recognisable dangerous industries – these included factories, explosives and mining inspectorates – while 'efficiency inspectorates' for public services – including the police and, from 1938, the fire service – were formed to maintain uniform standards of provision.[12] This chapter takes its cue from this established scholarship, as well as recent histories of deregulation of public utilities, in tracing three successive eras of building regulatory control in England and Wales.[13] While these eras overlapped one another, each was governed by a predominant regulatory framework. Each era inherited built forms according to pre-existing regulations, so they cannot be seen as marking a clear break from

[10] See, eg, Daniel Stedman Jones, *Masters of the Universe: Hayek, Friedman, and the Birth of Neoliberal Politics* (Princeton, NJ: Princeton University Press, 2014); Ben Jackson, 'The Think Tank Archipelago: Thatcherism and Neo-Liberalism', in Ben Jackson and Robert Saunders, eds., *Making Thatcher's Britain* (Cambridge: Cambridge University Press, 2012), 43–61.

[11] Majone, 'Paradoxes', 54; Steve Tombs, *Social Protection after the Crisis: Regulation without Enforcement* (Bristol: Policy Press, 2017).

[12] Oliver Macdonagh, 'The Nineteenth-Century Revolution in Government: A Reappraisal', *Historical Journal* 1, no. 1 (1958): 52–67; Jill Pellew, 'The Home Office and the Explosives Act of 1875', *Victorian Studies* 18, no. 2 (1974): 175–94; Gerald Rhodes, *Inspectorates in British Government: Law Enforcement and Standards of Efficiency* (London: Allen and Unwin, 1981); Roy MacLeod, ed., *Government and Expertise: Specialists, Administrators and Professionals, 1860–1919* (Cambridge: Cambridge University Press, 1988).

[13] Judith Clifton, Pierre Lanthier and Harm Schröter, 'Regulating and Deregulating the Public Utilities 1830–2010', *Business History* 53, no. 5 (2011): 659–72. While the experience of building control in Scotland and Northern Ireland clearly fell within these waves, they were subject to their own specific legislative regimes and regulatory bodies, which it is not possible to cover here in detail.

past practice, but rather evolved gradually, subject to pressures to reform from within, often drawn from different ideological, professional and political backgrounds. The first era involved the framing and codification of rules governing building in order to tackle the debilitating health effects of urbanisation and industrialisation between roughly the 1840s and 1920s, but the antecedents of this can be traced back to the seventeenth century. This regulatory era was noted for its diverse practices in enforcement and compliance, with larger metropolitan areas taking a lead in developing a more rigorous *local* system of building control. The second era, straddling the period from the 1930s to the 1970s, saw building control, for a brief moment, take on *national* significance. The phased introduction of uniform regulations based on prescriptive 'deemed to satisfy' criteria aimed to improve standards of construction as well as the health and safety of building users.

The third era, that of deregulation, began in the late 1970s and symbolically culminated with the Grenfell fire in 2017. As an Independent Review of Building Regulations and Fire Safety subsequently revealed, these roughly four decades heralded a shift in responsibility for building compliance away from the state and onto the individual, otherwise known as the 'responsible person'. While the author of this review, Judith Hackitt, made several recommendations for improvements to their enforcement in the wake of the fire, the Building Regulations themselves (including their supporting documents) have not been subject to any substantive changes. In this sense, the third and first eras share similarities in terms of the flexibility of controls in permitting varying standards and types of building construction, as well as in enabling arm's-length regulation by central government, but remain distinct because the third era embedded greater choice into the regulatory regime and this continues to be the defining feature of the system post-Grenfell. The second era, on the other hand, briefly established stronger regulatory control by central and local government, with clearer options for enforcement by local authority building control and fire brigades. Each era is thus marked by different emphases on the degree of participation of the state and the market in the governance of safety.

The onset of public health regulation

In September 1666 fire raged across London, devouring property in the City. King Charles II's subsequent proclamation paved the way for the introduction of byelaws, described by Clingan as 'our first building regulations of national significance'.[14] The byelaws transformed the City's built form in two ways:

---

[14] Clingan, 'National Building Regulations', 206.

first, by stipulating the use of brick or stone for rebuilding houses, with fixed thickness and height of walls; and second, by widening streets with greater distances between frontages in order to limit fire spread. From 1774, faced with the challenge of housing a growing population, the first statutory surveyors were appointed with powers to enforce compliance with London's byelaws.[15]

Between 1800 and 1845 almost 400 local improvement acts dealing with building and sanitary control were approved in England and Wales. However, despite the statistical evidence confirming the link between mortality, sanitation and housing conditions in industrial towns, calls for a national building act went unheeded. Opponents, many of whom were landlords, objected to the argument that national legislation would benefit communities on the grounds that it interfered with prevailing *laissez-faire* thinking. They also warned that building control would threaten their proprietary rights and increase housing costs, which they threatened to pass on to renters, establishing a longstanding precedent that has been frequently invoked in recent years to reject calls for tougher controls over the housing market.[16] Subsequent legislation retained the principle that building control would remain permissive and be administered primarily at local level, which meant that improvements to the quality of building remained patchy. Although the 1848 Public Health Act introduced oversight from central government, boroughs jealously guarded their powers to self-govern.[17]

The principle had thus been established that regulatory reform would be piecemeal, discretionary and consolidatory, following the path of least intervention. A centralised public health regime, created during the 1870s, established the first comprehensive administrative system, with accompanying building codes, incorporating wider areas of control designed to improve the public's health. The creation of the Local Government Board (LGB) in 1871 standardised control and raised the status of surveyors within local government. The landmark 1875 Public Health Act consolidated previous legislation and granted powers to local authorities to frame byelaws for promoting public health and preventing fires. Two years later, the LGB issued

---

[15] C.C. Knowles and P.H. Pitt, *The History of Building Regulation in London 1189–1972* (London: Architectural Press, 1972), 30–5, 49–54.

[16] Roger Harper, *Victorian Building Regulations* (London: Mansell, 1985), xiii–xiv; S.M. Gaskell, *Building Control: National Legislation and the Introduction of Local Bye-Laws in Victorian England* (London: Bedford Square Press, 1983), 6–12.

[17] Royston Lambert, 'Central and Local Relations in Mid-Victorian England: The Local Government Act Office, 1858–71', *Victorian Studies* 6, no. 2 (1962): 121–50.

model byelaws to encourage local authorities to raise the standard of house-building; London was again excluded from these provisions. By 1882, over 1,500 sets of byelaws had been approved, albeit retaining significant local variations.[18]

London continued to be governed by its own building codes, administered from 1855 by the Metropolitan Board of Works and, from 1889, the London County Council (LCC). One of the LCC's first tasks was to secure an updated Building Act to establish controls over the growing fashion for taller buildings, which it did in 1894 with the support of professional bodies such as the Royal Institute of British Architects (RIBA). The Act also introduced a greater range of clauses regulating building height, which was set at 80 feet to reflect the maximum length to which the Metropolitan (later renamed London) Fire Brigade's escape ladders could extend.[19]

The regulatory system was subjected to increasing pressure to standardise in the aftermath of the First World War. In 1918, the report of a Departmental Committee on Building Byelaws recommended government introduce a national code to expire every ten years, thereby requiring local authorities to adopt up-to-date model byelaws.[20] The case for stronger controls was overridden by the urgent demand for new housing, however, especially in the light of Prime Minister David Lloyd George's 'homes fit for heroes' speech in 1918. With shortages of materials and skilled builders, government instead advocated the continuation of the existing system of byelaws. The Housing and Town Planning Act 1919 established a greater role for the state in subsidising builders to construct model housing. Any major reform of building control was put on hold for much of the inter-war period until the system was brought onto a national footing on the eve of war. It also incorporated the definitions of a 1932 British Standard for 'fire resistance', stipulating that roofs, walls and floors 'shall possess a degree of fire-resistance appropriate to the purpose for which the building is intended to be used'.[21] From 1939 local authorities were required to make their own byelaws for all new buildings, based on the model series overseen by the Ministry of Health, although policymakers remained sensitive to accusations of overregulation. But a consensus had been reached within

[18] Gaskell, *Building Control*, 42–8; Harper, *Victorian Building*, xix–xx, xxii.
[19] Knowles and Pitt, *Building Regulation in London*, 73–7, 86–94.
[20] Anthony James Ley, 'Building Control: Its Development and Application 1840–1936', Open University MPhil, 1990, 156–63.
[21] G.E. Mitchell, *Model Building Byelaws Illustrated*, 2nd edition (London: B.T. Batsford, 1947), 34.

Whitehall that a discretionary system produced inconsistent checks and balances; the path of least intervention was about to take a decisive, but reversible, diversion.

The emergence of national regulation

The conditions were ripe for creating national building regulations in the years that followed the end of the Second World War. A 1952 revision of byelaws introduced two advances. Firstly, 'deemed to satisfy' provisions were combined with 'standards of performance' to allow 'the utmost possible freedom in building methods provided the functional requirements are satisfied'.[22] Greater flexibility was designated 'in the national interest on account of the housing shortage and in order to stay apace of the needs of modern industry'.[23] George Clingan's bold prediction had come to fruition two years before his retirement after fifty-two years' public service.[24]

Secondly, the 1952 byelaws contained more precise assessment of fire risk by specifying fire resistance periods in relation to building type and size based on the findings of the wartime government's fire grading committee. This established the principle of compartmentation within large buildings with shared access routes. Integrating approved walls, floors, doors and windows into a building's passive defence heralded a major shift in firefighting policy, providing for the safe exit of occupants while assisting firefighters in their work. It also led to the adoption of a British Standard Code of Practice in 1962, which established the 'stay put' fire service strategy for higher-risk residential buildings (HRRBs).[25] These changes, alongside the relaxation of rules concerning maximum building height, incentivised the construction industry to embrace new industrialised building systems, including high-rise flats, as part of the state's housing boom of the 1950s and 1960s. The greater expense of construction materials and state subsidy would be offset by lower site and labour costs; additional savings were offered in the provision that only stipulated a single internal staircase for means of escape in case of fire in all tall buildings that exceeded the fire brigade's rescue height.[26]

[22] Ministry of Housing and Local Government, *Model Bye-Laws, Series IV: Buildings* (London: HMSO, 1952), 3.

[23] Patrick Dunleavy, *The Politics of Mass Housing in Britain, 1945–1975: A Study of Corporate Power and Professional Influence in the Welfare State* (Oxford: Clarendon Press, 1981), 60.

[24] *Liverpool Echo*, 1 September 1954, 12.

[25] *British Standard Code of Practice CP 3: Chapter IV: Precautions Against Fire. Part 1: Flats and Maisonettes (in blocks over two storeys)* (London: British Standards Institution, 1978), 5.

[26] The National Archives (hereafter TNA) HLG/51/1117, 'Means of Escape from Flats and Maisonettes', July 1954; Miles Glendinning and Stefan Muthesius, *Tower Block:*

National regulation had thus been adopted within central government as an administrative instrument for enforcing improved construction standards by the 1960s. The 1961 Public Health Act offered the opportunity to extend executive responsibility, removing from local authorities powers to make their own byelaws and centralising them within the Ministry of Housing and Local Government (MHLG), a forerunner of the Department for Communities and Local Government[27] which presided over the regulations in 2017. In its spirit, then, the 1961 Act represented the culmination of a longer-term shift in building control, relegating local authorities to the status of agents of central government policy in all cities with the exception of London where the LCC retained discretionary powers.

To ensure that statutory requirements kept pace with technical advances, the 1961 Act appointed an advisory body of professionals working across the construction industries and the fire service. While the higher civil service had long drawn on the expertise of scientists, the 1960s heralded a 'technocratic moment' for British social and political life in which specialists were consulted by governments to benefit daily life in a variety of mundane but essential ways, as we shall explore in the next chapter.[28] First meeting in 1962, and reporting two years later, the Building Regulations Advisory Committee kept the regulations under constant review, working closely with partners in the Fire and Rescue Service and other government agencies. Initially located within the MHLG, it was transferred to the Ministry of Public Buildings and Works in 1964 before returning to the MHLG three years later, eventually settling in the Department of the Environment (DoE) in 1970.[29] Multiple 'machinery of government' changes – a theme we shall return to later – reveal the tensions between ministerial interest in matters of building control and the heavy administrative burden imposed on civil servants and their advisory bodies to keep up to date with specialist professional practice.

Modern Public Housing in England, Scotland, Wales and Northern Ireland (New Haven, CT: Yale University Press, 1994), 62; Peter Scott, 'Friends in High Places: Government-Industry Relations in Public Sector House-Building during Britain's Tower Block Era', *Business History* 62, no. 4 (2020): 545–65.

[27] Since renamed the Ministry of Housing, Communities and Local Government in 2018 and, in 2021, the Department for Levelling Up, Housing and Communities.

[28] David Edgerton, *The Rise and Fall of the British Nation: A Twentieth-Century History* (London: Penguin, 2019), 400–1.

[29] TNA WORK/75/32, 'Building Regulations Advisory Committee First Report', Cmd. 2279 (London: HMSO, 1964); TNA WORK/75/33, 'Research and Testing: Action Arising'.

The Building Regulations came into operation in 1966, two years after their approval by ministers.[30] Their principal objective was to extend the model byelaws across England and Wales, with the exception of that part of London under the administration of the new Greater London Council (GLC).[31] As with the Victorian public health reforms, the introduction of national regulations was never intended to be the end of the story. In the twenty years following their introduction, they were consolidated twice and amended fourteen times, before they were 'recast' in 1985. While predominantly of an administrative nature, the amendments reflected the changed priorities of government towards the modernisation of social infrastructure as well as its wider commitment to protecting public safety. The 1970s, far from being a decade of political inertia as they are commonly and erroneously described, were a time of continued refinement and improvement to public safety, as recent histories have revealed.[32]

Three main amendments were introduced at the start of the decade. First, metric regulations were approved in 1972, in readiness for Britain's entry into the Common Market the following year.[33] Second, an amendment in 1970 introduced new rules for controlling the design of buildings over five storeys high in order to give structural protection against accidental loads. This was in response to the Ronan Point gas explosion in May 1968. The Tribunal of Inquiry rebuked the Labour Government for its top-down managerialist approach and called for the block's strengthening.[34] Thirdly, the 1965 regulations had not specified means of escape in its precautions. This omission was corrected with the 1971 Fire Precautions Act, which forms the focus of the next chapter, and a 1973 amendment stipulated the provision of exits and escape routes in larger multi-storey buildings. The 1973 amendment was a response to the Summerland leisure centre disaster earlier that year on the Isle of Man. This tragedy, with fifty deaths and eighty serious injuries, including many young children, revealed systemic failures

---

[30] The Building Regulations followed Scotland's example, which had been put on a national footing in 1959; Northern Ireland followed in 1972.

[31] London was incorporated into the Regulations in 1986 following the GLC's abolition.

[32] See, eg, chapters in Crook and Esbester, *Governing Risks*; Lawrence Black, Hugh Pemberton and Pat Thane, eds., *Reassessing 1970s Britain* (Manchester: Manchester University Press, 2013).

[33] W.S. Whyte and Vincent Powell-Smith, *The Building Regulations Explained and Illustrated for Residential Buildings*, 4th edition (London: Crosby, Lockwood & Son, 1972), vii.

[34] TNA HLG/118/1133, 'Building Regulations Advisory Committee, Sub-committee to consider proposals for 5th amendment to Building Regulations'.

in building control and sent shockwaves reverberating across Britain.[35] It has subsequently been cited by several experts as evidence of the British state's and industry's blindness to learning from historic multiple-fatality events in the aftermath of the Grenfell fire, including the Hackitt Review.[36] Indeed, in their closing submissions to Phase 1 of the public inquiry, counsel representing the bereaved and survivors cited Summerland as one of 'The Fires That Foretold Grenfell', with one claiming that, although 'it led in the short-term to the strengthening of outdated Building Regulations in the UK, the lessons were not learnt by the powers that be' and, by the early 1980s, 'the deregulation of fire safety was in full swing'.[37]

These are bold claims but not without merit. Even before the special commission of inquiry had been tasked with investigating the tragedy, newspapers asked questions of the Douglas Corporation, which had approved the architect's application to allow the approximately 50,000-square-foot frontage to be clad in Oroglas, a combustible acrylic glass sheeting which had never been subjected to testing. The fire, which was accidentally started by three boys smoking in a disused kiosk on the miniature golf course, soon ignited the eastern end of the main building, itself clad in another flammable material called Galbestos, made from plastic-coated steel sheeting. The flames quickly engulfed the Galbestos sheeting and, spreading through poorly fireproofed vents, ignited the acrylic roof, sending burning chunks of molten plastic falling onto holidaymakers as they evacuated. A three-and-a-half-acre 'dream complex', marketed as 'Britain's first forget-the-weather family fun centre', was reduced 'so swiftly and so hopelessly into a blazing death trap' and the centre's designers, builders and regulators were all implicated in its failure.[38]

A scathing front-page editorial in the *Daily Mirror*, which echoes similar pieces published in the days following the Grenfell Tower fire,[39] blasted those who had failed to protect holidaying families:

---

[35] The fire and its aftermath are detailed in Ian Phillips, 'The Summerland Fire Disaster' (2020), available at <https://www.summerlandfiredisaster.co.uk, accessed 7 March 2023>.

[36] Hackitt, *Interim Report*, 32; Kernick, *Catastrophe*, 29.

[37] GTI, Closing submissions from Counsel Rajiv Menon and Michael Mansfield QC, 11 December 2018, 24, 65–6.

[38] *Daily Mail*, 4 August 1973, 1; *The Guardian*, 9 August 1973, 6.

[39] A selection of newspaper headlines was compiled by *The Guardian*, 15 June 2017, <https://www.theguardian.com/uk-news/gallery/2017/jun/15/newspapers-around-the -world-react-to-the-grenfell-tower-fire-in-pictures>. Please note that they include graphic images of the tower in flames.

New types of plastic material are constantly being put on the market. They may be safe. They may not. They may be safe under some conditions. But not under others. The responsibility lies heavily on the Government, on every local authority, on every architect, on every builder to ensure that no material is used that has not been independently tested ... In the year 1973 it should be possible to guarantee that no fire will spread with the terrifying speed of the one that engulfed Summerland.[40]

Yet the borough council waived its byelaws in order to allow the use of Galbestos and Oroglas to reduce costs and create an artificial sunshine palace. Aesthetic and financial considerations were prioritised at the expense of safety in the most flagrant abuse of regulations since their introduction, which, as the Grenfell Inquiry reminds us, demonstrates that governments must be held accountable for their failure to protect those who are most vulnerable to fire.

While fire industry experts reassured tourists in England and Wales that the 'construction of such a building as the Summerland holiday complex would be unlikely to be allowed in this country', alarm bells inevitably rang loudly, particularly in the light of several fires at domestic holiday camps, including Butlins' complex at Pwllheli a few days later. Anxiety was heightened as fire industry organisations voiced their concerns at the omission of means of escape provisions from the regulations: 'When will the British accept the urgent need for adequate fire risk control?', asked the *Financial Times*.[41] No time soon, it would appear, as the government rejected recommendations to strengthen existing laws, insisting that local authorities already had sufficient licensing powers. Instead, Home Office officials, in remaining on the path of least intervention, drew up a voluntary code of guidance for the 1975 holiday season.[42] The Summerland Fire Commission agreed, concluding from its investigations that the disaster was the result of 'many human errors and failures', but called for greater controls over exterior as well as interior features to reduce the risk of external fire spread.[43] As for the leisure centre's architect, he was exonerated from

[40] *Daily Mirror*, 4 August 1973, 1.

[41] *Financial Times*, 10 August 1973, 11; 4 August 1973, 24.

[42] TNA AY/21/24/CP74/74, 'Report on the Spread of Fire at Summerland, Douglas, Isle of Man', 2 August 1973; *Report of Her Majesty's Chief Inspector of Fire Services for the Year 1974*, Cmd. 6145, 23.

[43] J.D. Cantlie et al., *Report of the Summerland Fire Commission* (Isle of Man: Government Office, 1974), 77. The Commission's findings regarding external fire spread were submitted by the Fire Brigades Union to the public inquiry: GTI, FBU00000130_Exhibit MW 99, 12 March 2022.

accusations of professional misconduct and retired to live on his yacht off Corfu.[44]

These disasters, and the subsequent regulatory changes they triggered, occurred at a crucial moment in the state's provision of health and safety. Whereas governments had responded to accidents at work with more prescriptive regulations since the 1950s, there had been no subsequent diminishing of danger. In fact, the number of workplace deaths and injuries increased during the 1950s and 1960s, which pointed to the limitations of a reactive system of regulation. Rather than restricting worker freedoms, so it was thought, the state would be better off empowering employees to accept greater responsibility for their individual safety in order to get a grip on the problem. In 1970 a committee of inquiry, led by the former chair of the National Coal Board Lord Robens, was appointed to review health and safety provision in the workplace. Robens's report, and the resultant legislation, forwarded the notion that occupational safety was the responsibility of employees and employers as well as the state. Workplace health and safety would be managed by a series of 'functional regulations' that specified the desired objective rather than the means to get there. This heralded a new era of self-regulation within a statutory framework composed of voluntary codes of practice developed within industry and by individual bodies. From now on, the state would regulate from afar, with responsibility passing onto the individual and, in certain instances, to professional associations such as the Fire Brigades Union.[45]

The 1974 Health and Safety at Work etc. Act was at odds with the 'deemed to satisfy' provisions contained in the Building Regulations. Criticism of the heavy-handed regulations was ramped up in the context of the light-touch approach preferred by Lord Robens. Political support for greater levels of self-regulation echoed a discourse of anti-red-tapeism within the popular media, which had intensified over the previous decade. Some of this criticism was evidently politicised. Writing in 1964, Peter Whalley, the *Daily Mail*'s property writer, welcomed the 1959–64 Conservative Government's draft regulations on the grounds that they promised to cut the cost of building the average home as well as encourage the construction of schools and hospitals.[46] Yet within two years, Whalley was bemoaning the same regulations for failing to improve standards and innovation, for

---

[44] *Daily Telegraph*, 31 July 1979, 15.

[45] Paul Almond and Mike Esbester, *Health and Safety in Contemporary Britain: Society, Legitimacy, and Change since 1960* (Basingstoke: Palgrave Macmillan, 2019); Modern Records Centre, MSS.346/4/149, 'Health and Safety Guidelines for Firefighters'.

[46] *Daily Mail*, 28 February 1964, 11.

which he blamed the Labour Government's failure to rein in surveyors. Only by separating building inspection from local government and regulating it through industry bodies would standards be improved, according to Whalley.[47]

Following Margaret Thatcher's election as leader of the Conservative Party in 1975, media criticism became more trenchant. Daniel Stedman Jones has noted the important role played by newspaper journalists in espousing neoliberal ideas such as monetarism and free trade during the 1970s, and the same can be said about support for the deregulation of building control, with polemical writers citing bureaucratic bottlenecks and excessive costs as inhibiting the rights of homeowners to change their homes without repeatedly clashing with fussy inspectors armed with clipboards and prohibition notices.[48] The *Daily Mail*, the most hostile newspaper, regularly published 'puff pieces' about the ease and convenience of home extensions, loft conversions and the installation of new heating systems, under such headlines as 'You don't have to move to own a larger house' and 'When staying put could be your best move …'. While such pieces identify various loopholes in the existing law, they also warn the reader to check with the local authority to avoid being 'tied down by red tape', as one middle-aged couple found with their idea for a 'dream home' in Essex. The couple's plans for a farm conversion were repeatedly blocked by planners working for the local council who 'object to every little detail – even the size of the windows'. Four years on, the family were still living in a caravan on the property, their plans on hold.[49]

Recasting the Building Regulations

In 1979 a Conservative government led by Margaret Thatcher was elected on a pledge to introduce greater choice for the individual by undoing many of the reforms of the post-war period. With the goal to cut public expenditure and reduce economic controls, government set out to shrink the state rather than continue the post-war trend for expanding responsibilities in the interrelated fields of welfare, health and safety provision. This marked a new era of building regulation, that of deregulation, during which the fire at Grenfell Tower occurred. This era is marked by a diminished role for the state and an increased role for the private sector and property developers to self-regulate in the absence of what popular newspapers and politicians

[47] *Daily Mail*, 7 March 1966, 8.
[48] Stedman Jones, *Masters of the Universe*, 233–5.
[49] *Daily Mail*, 10 February 1973, 25; 26 May 1973, 20; 25 August 1973, 22; 15 May 1976, 14.

increasingly derided as unnecessary state controls. As we shall see in the next chapter, this era of deregulation also saw the erosion of the law on fire precautions, with responsibility for safety passing from the state to the individual.

The Thatcher Government's approach towards 'recasting' the Building Regulations can be understood in the context of two broad developments; first, the late twentieth-century shift from social democracy to market liberalism, which saw her appeal to a growing popular individualism among voters; second, her party's longstanding support for a 'property-owning democracy'. This led to 'the largest transfer of property from the state to the individual' in the country's history as 'a new type of citizen', the working-class homeowner who was more likely to be aligned with traditional Conservative voters, emerged as a key voter. Thatcher's government was elected on a promise to roll back 'the frontiers of the state' by selling off state assets and reducing public debt while also offering greater choice to those people who were increasingly confident in staking a claim to their rights and identities. Publicly owned utilities were seen as an obstacle to efficiency, removing the incentive to innovate and deliver improved services at a lower price to the 'consumer'. As a result, policymakers advocated that public services should be subject to competition from the market to encourage them to operate more economically and efficiently.[50] The 'Right to Buy' programme, introduced in 1980, gave council house tenants who had rented for three years or more the right to buy their homes at a significant discount of the market value; eventually this became 'the largest single privatisation of public goods' at an estimated value of £2 billion by 1997.[51]

Just as supporters of 'Right to Buy' cited the importance of 'choice' for tenants to own their own homes, so too did these arguments dominate the building control sector. As several expert witnesses have testified to the Grenfell Inquiry, the new secretary of state for the environment, Michael Heseltine, 'fired the starting gun for the policy of deregulation in the construction industry' that culminated with the 2017 fire.[52] While Heseltine's

[50] Matthew Francis, '"A Crusade to Enfranchise the Many": Thatcherism and the Property-Owning Democracy', *Twentieth Century British History* 23, no. 2 (2012): 275–97; E. Robinson et al., 'Telling Stories about Post-War Britain: Popular Individualism and the "Crisis" of the 1970s', *Twentieth Century British History* 28, no. 2 (2017): 268–304; Guy Ortolano, *Thatcher's Progress: From Social Democracy to Market Liberalism through an English New Town* (Cambridge: Cambridge University Press, 2019).

[51] Francis, 'Crusade', 295.

[52] See, eg, GTI, Martin Seaward and Nick Toms, 'FBU00000191_Phase 2 Module 6 Part 2 – Written Closing Submission on behalf of the Fire Brigades Union', 6 June 2022,

promise to 'reduce the nannying and overseeing' of local authorities by Whitehall pleased professional associations exasperated by 'the nightmare of bureaucratic control', for Heseltine, sweeping away 'expensive and time-consuming' controls translated into diminished responsibilities for local authorities and greater levels of competition between the state and market.[53] Indeed, 'far from giving local government more freedom there may, in fact, be worse to come', noted the *Municipal Journal*, which warned that local authorities were entering a new decade shackled 'in chains' amidst threats to cut public expenditure and introduce rate capping.[54]

In December 1979, Heseltine pledged to take 'a hard look' at the system of building control in a speech to the National House-Building Council (NHBC), a private consumer watchdog that had long advocated for greater freedom for housebuilders. 'I am not in the business of just tinkering with the problem', he insisted; he was committed to creating a simplified system, the main thrust of which would involve reducing the role of local authorities and granting greater responsibility to private providers with the ultimate aim of making building control self-financing and self-regulating: 'There are strong arguments for a system of control which embodies the principle that anyone who carries out work, or causes it to be carried out, should be responsible for the outcome.'[55] While simplifying the language of the Building Regulations was welcomed across the sector, Heseltine's proposal for greater self-regulation by the construction industry met with disapproval from building control inspectors who wanted a greater measure of independence themselves. What was needed, wrote the Institution of Municipal Engineers (IME), were 'suitably qualified practitioners' to ensure that the primary objective of building control remains 'the effective protection of the health and safety of the public' and not the reduction of controls.[56]

A government consultation document, published in 1980, outlined options for simplifying the system and reducing its burden on the taxpayer. These included 'recasting' regulation as a minimum number of functional requirements only; exempting local authorities from control; and introducing certification by approved private persons as an alternative to local authority control. A white paper consequently proposed a combination

---

3; GTI LBYP20000001/52, Professor Luke Bisby, 'Phase 2 – Regulatory Testing and the Path of Grenfell', 10 November 2021, 1132.

[53] *MJ*, 4 May 1979, 451.

[54] *MJ*, 18 May 1979, 503; 25 May 1979, 543; 21 December 1979, 1339.

[55] *Financial Times*, 4 December 1979, 7; 11 December 1979, 6.

[56] *MJ*, 14 December 1979, 1303–5; *Chartered Municipal Engineer* (*CME*), March 1980, 64.

of all three options by widening exemptions and introducing certification that provided for greater self-regulation by construction professionals.[57] Unsurprisingly, the NHBC, which had been lobbying for powers to act as a certifying authority, welcomed the proposals, seeing them as beneficial for homeowners. RIBA also welcomed the reforms as freeing its members from the costs of building control. The Institute of Building Control and the local authority associations expressed concern at the intended fragmentation of responsibility and loss of revenue, while also warning that private firms would poach 'competent persons' from local authorities with the offer of competitive rates of pay. Minimum self-regulation 'would obviously lower standards', warned one surveyor, who noted that multiple-fatality disasters occurred in buildings outside the scope of regulatory controls, as was seen in the case of the Summerland fire. Other commercial bodies, including the Royal Institution of Chartered Surveyors (RICS), predicted that the proposals could lead to a sharp increase in the cost of insurance, with many landlords passing these on to tenants or leaseholders, which is precisely what happened in the wake of the unfolding cladding crisis following the 2017 Grenfell fire.[58]

Proposals for the simplification of the regulations were issued in 1982. The main proposal – to shift from 'deemed to satisfy' clauses to open-ended functional regulations – was welcomed by housing providers and industry bodies. In general, local authority groups opposed the proposals, concerned at the loss of responsibility and revenue. Serious reservations were raised by fire safety organisations. In a warning that later bore fruit, the Institution of Fire Engineers (IFE), whose core membership was composed of firefighters, warned that the new form 'will give Architects much greater freedom and enforcing authorities much less control and much greater difficulty in enforcing "Safe" performance standards'. In particular, the IFE warned that 'the expertise and experience of the Fire Authority in matters relating to fire is recognised and should not be lost', indicating that no building control authority should approve plans until they received from the fire authority a safety certificate, yet this is precisely what the government introduced.[59]

Undeterred by the criticism, and bolstered by a larger majority following the 1983 general election, the government's Housing and Building Control

---

[57] DoE, *White Paper on the Future of Building Control in England and Wales*, Cmd. 8179 (London: HMSO, 1981).

[58] *Financial Times*, 6 October 1980, 42; *MJ*, 11 January 1980, 27–8; *MJ*, 8 August 1980, 994–5; *CME*, September 1980, 209–16.

[59] TNA AT/49/161, 'Building Regulations Reform, Summaries of Responses to Consultation', 30 March 1983.

Bill was passed the following year. In addition to extending the provisions of its 'Right to Buy' programme, the Act introduced competition into building oversight. Under regulations issued the following year, it allowed for privately certified building inspectors, including the NHBC, to compete for contracts. The government's pro-market sentiments continued in its subsequent attack on 'red tape', deploying the language popularised by newspapers by pledging to 'lift the burden' on small firms through the removal of a raft of regulations. In a 1985 report, 'Burdens of Business', by Secretary of State for Trade and Industry Lord George Young, building regulations were cited as one of the top ten 'burdens' placed upon small firms.[60] The subsequent white paper committed government to deregulation in order to achieve two aims: first, 'freeing markets and increasing the opportunities for competition' and, second, 'lifting administrative and legislative burdens which take time, energy and resources from fundamental business activity'. This would be achieved in two stages: by 'simplifying' existing regulations so that they afford greater 'freedom' and 'flexibility' to the building process, before establishing 'how far they can be reduced or dropped altogether' in order to reduce regulations 'to the minimum required to secure their essential function, which is the preservation of public health and safety'.[61]

Right-wing newspapers welcomed Young's proposals, with Robin Oakley in the *Daily Mail* gleefully reporting that '[m]asses of red tape and pettifogging regulations which hamper small firms are to be slashed away'. Similarly, Peter Hitchens, writing in the *Daily Express*, reported that government had gone to 'war on red tape', praising proposals to free businesses from 'needlessly elaborate regulations on safety and fire'.[62] More muted voices warned that cutting red tape could lead to more dangerous living and working conditions. *The Guardian* quoted Labour's Treasury spokesman, a young Tony Blair, who described the white paper as a 'shabby and irrelevant document ... whose ideology is unable to solve the problems of the economy', before seeking guarantees that the plans 'will not lead to loss of safety and fire regulations or environmental protection'.[63]

The recast Building Regulations, introduced in 1985, were described as 'the most radical shake-up of the building control system since the ...

---

[60] Department of Trade and Industry, *Burdens on Business: Report of a Scrutiny of Administrative and Legislative Requirements* (London: HMSO, 1985); *Financial Times*, 30 April 1985, 11.

[61] Minister without Portfolio, *Lifting the Burden*, Cmd. 9571 (London: HMSO, 1985), 15–16.

[62] *Daily Mail*, 17 July 1985, 9; *Daily Express*, 17 July 1985, 7.

[63] *The Guardian*, 17 July 1985, 1; *Daily Mirror*, 17 July 1985, 2.

establishment of the system of building bye-laws' in the Victorian period.[64] It can equally be argued that they heralded the beginnings of a diminution of public safety, or, in the words of Judith Hackitt, a 'race to the bottom' of a culture of building control that prioritised profit over safety through ignorance or indifference.[65] Other than for means of escape in case of fire, functional requirements were introduced, which stated the aim of the regulation rather than the means of achieving the requirement. Even then, government was committed to 'reducing the level of regulation in these areas, where this would not lead to increased risk to personal safety'. Critics of the regulations had increasingly bemoaned the length of the published regulations, which they complained had been allowed to 'breed like rabbits' by successive governments. As one author noted:

> In the bad, dangerous past of pre-1965 we had 78 pages of regulations. The year of 1965, when regulations were nationalised, these became 168 pages. The take-off point started in 1972. There are now over 350 pages, and even more are breeding in the department's hutches.[66]

Thatcher's government added to the number of regulations it inherited; it took intervention in order to deregulate. In 1980 a scale of fees was introduced for building control in order to bring about public expenditure savings of £40 million. Critics, however, warned that fees would 'do nothing to ease the present climate of dissatisfaction with which building control officers have to cope' and would contribute to enhanced client expectations for building approval.[67] Moreover, while later controls were introduced to ensure adequate access for disabled persons, these were not seen to deflect attention away from the more radical changes of providing for private certification and removing 'unnecessary regulations'. Indeed, Thatcher's government slavishly culled its own breeding programme, reducing three hundred and ten pages of specific regulations supported by twelve detailed schedules to twenty-four pages comprising twenty functional regulations and three schedules.[68] Yet the detail did not disappear, as twelve booklets of advisory guidance, known as Approved Documents, were introduced, including one booklet – Approved Document B – dealing entirely with

---

[64] A.J. Ley, *A History of Building Control in England and Wales 1840–1990* (Coventry: RICS Books, 2000), 141.

[65] Hackitt, *Final Report*, 5.

[66] *Daily Telegraph*, 30 January 1980, 11.

[67] *CME*, March 1980, 61; *MJ*, 11 April 1980, 454–5.

[68] *Lifting the Burden*, 15–16.

structural fire safety. 'So much for cutting red tape', noted the authors of a recent history.[69]

This published guidance went through several revisions from 1992 under Conservative and New Labour governments alike. While the 1991 and 1992 revisions updated fire safety features, they opened up more areas of building control to private operators, extending a process that had started a decade earlier. This inevitably led to greater fragmentation of regulatory control.[70] Further revisions, introduced in 2000, endorsed large-scale fire testing of external cladding systems alongside greater choice for construction product manufacturers in satisfying the regulations, especially as they pertained to taller buildings. To cope with the growing workload of testing, the New Labour Government later permitted the widespread use of 'full-scale test data'.[71] In practice, this meant that use of combustible materials was permitted under certain conditions, in particular for insulating buildings with exterior wall cladding, while an ever-shrinking pool of fire prevention officers meant that enforcement was patchy at best. Deregulation established the legal right, if not the moral legitimacy, of developers to prioritise the costs of development over and above those of the safety of a building's occupants. So much for learning lessons; successive 'machinery of government' changes since the 1990s meant that responsible ministries like the DoE and its successors had forgotten the horrors of earlier cladding fires such as Summerland.

Matters came to a head following the Grenfell Tower fire with the formation of the Hackitt Review. Issuing her final report in 2018, Hackitt concluded that the regulatory system was 'not fit for purpose' and called for 'a radical rethink' of the whole system, including the creation of a regulatory framework and a building safety regulator, managed by the Health and Safety Executive (HSE), with responsibility to oversee the safety and performance of HRRBs. The construction industry had failed to reflect and learn for itself, and it had not looked to other sectors for guidance. What is required, Hackitt and other commentators write, is a culture change in the industry from top to bottom. While Hackitt's report and the government's subsequent response have signalled a return to the collaborative approach

---

[69] Prosser and Taylor, *Grenfell Tower Fire*, 101; Department of the Environment, *The Building Regulations 1985: Approved Document B – Fire Spread* (London: HMSO, 1985). Approved Document B has gone through multiple revisions, the most recent of which was in 2019, with amendments in 2020 and 2022: <https://www.gov.uk/government /publications/fire-safety-approved-document-b>.

[70] *MJ*, 23 January 1992, 16–17.

[71] Prosser and Taylor, *Grenfell Tower Fire*, 102–3.

championed in earlier eras of regulation, it nominally goes further in advocating a stronger voice for residents, which has since been adopted by the HSE in the Regulator's governance. It remains to be seen how far residents' concerns will be taken seriously, which has led to a number of campaigners calling upon the government and its regulatory bodies 'to ensure the voices of those with less power are both heard and count'.[72] The signs do not bode well: the Conservative Government's Fire Safety Act, finally passed in 2021, angered many campaigners for reneging on its 2019 assurance to implement all of the recommendations issued in the Grenfell Inquiry Phase 1 report, 'in full' and 'without delay'.[73] One such recommendation, that mobility-impaired residents be supplied with Personal Emergency Evacuation Plans (PEEPs) to assist them in evacuating a building in an emergency, was rejected by the government following a cost–benefit analysis on the grounds of 'practicality', 'proportionality' and 'safety', including concerns that evacuation 'might hinder firefighting strategy'.[74] Yet the fact that mobility-impaired residents face a disproportionate risk to their lives from fires in high-rise buildings – 40 per cent of the disabled residents living in Grenfell Tower died in the 2017 fire – has been cited by campaigners as proof of the government's failure to protect those who are forced to live in a perpetual state of vulnerability owing to their inability to self-evacuate. Evidently the 'excessive costs' cited of introducing robust safety measures continue to override the government's priority for public safety.[75]

Conclusion

The long road to the Building Regulations radically switched direction from the 1980s, returning to a quasi-Victorian model of discretionary powers and greater freedoms for property developers and construction product manufacturers to act in their own interests. Historians can only speculate on what a surveyor like George Pierce Clingan, who spent more than four decades working within local government, would have made of this policy reversal after decades of effective regulation. In this we are assisted by

---

[72] Hackitt, *Final Report*, 5, 12; Kernick, *Catastrophe*, 147, 159.

[73] *Inside Housing*, 30 October 2019, <https://www.insidehousing.co.uk/news/news/government-to-implement-grenfell-inquiry-recommendations-in-full-and-provide-funding-63963>.

[74] Home Office, *Personal Emergency Evacuation Plans in High-Rise Residential Buildings – Recommendations from the Grenfell Tower Inquiry Phase 1 Report: Government Response* (London: HMSO, 2022), 53; Hansard (Lords), 25 May 2022, 847–50.

[75] See the joint letter from Disability Rights UK, Grenfell United and Claddag (the Leaseholder Disability Action Group) to the prime minister, 12 June 2022, at <https://www.disabilityrightsuk.org/news/2022/june/grenfell-5-years>, accessed 21 October 2022.

the written responses from professional bodies to the consultation on the recasting of the regulations in 1983. Whereas elements of the proposals were welcomed – not least the simplification and clarity given to their wording – warnings echoed from across the associations at the importance of providing training to building control officers to cope with the anticipated changes to site inspection and the introduction of Approved Documents (one body recommended the award of a 'certificate of competence' to building surveyors not dissimilar to RICS's call following the introduction of controversial EWS1 surveys for High-Rise Residential Buildings in 2019[76]). Moreover, several bodies – including the IME and IAAS[77] – reminded the DoE of the importance of ensuring that every residential building, including temporary accommodation provided at hotels, boarding houses and hostels, should have at least one means of escape in the event of fire in order to assist the work of the fire service as well as evacuation in instances where 'stay put' was inadvisable. Only with the retention of existing laws governing the provision of exits and entrances, as well as 'unequivocable wording' in the accompanying guidance, would the safety of residents and guests be subject to appropriate controls.[78] It is to the thorny issue of hotel precautions, as a window onto the wider theme of the deregulation of fire safety, that we now turn.

[76] RICS News, <https://www.rics.org/uk/news-insight/latest-news/fire-safety/cladding-qa>, accessed 7 March 2023.
[77] The IAAS was renamed the Association of Building Engineers in 1993, becoming the Chartered Association of Building Engineers in 2014. The IME merged with the Institution of Civil Engineers in 1984.
[78] TNA AT/49/161, 'Building Regulations Reform: Summaries of Responses', 30 March 1983.

2. How red tape saves lives: the law on fire precautions in Britain since the 1970s

The popular 1970s BBC sitcom *Fawlty Towers*, written by John Cleese and Connie Booth, is part of the national cultural imagination, well known for its satirising of the xenophobic little Englander and wartime nostalgia. Cleese's character, Basil Fawlty, the bumbling and unfriendly proprietor of the hotel, has even been described as a 'pre-Thatcherite' conservative.[1] A memorable scene, in the controversial episode 'The Germans', involves Basil dismally attempting to organise a scheduled fire drill. Through a series of mishaps involving a chip pan, his dim-witted waiter, Manuel (played by Andrew Sachs), sets his jacket alight and runs into the lobby yelling 'Is fire! Is fire!' Basil is incapable of operating the fire extinguisher, which explodes in his face, and it is left to Polly (played by Booth), the cool-headed chamber-maid, to save Manuel and the hotel. Basil is taken to hospital with concussion where he sets off on a typical rant, with a stinging reference to Harold Wilson, the Labour prime minister: 'It exploded in my face. I mean, what is the point of a fire extinguisher? It sits there for months, and when you actually have a fire, when you actually need the bloody thing, it blows your head off! I mean, what is happening to this country? It's bloody Wilson.'[2]

To Basil, holding a fire drill is an unwelcome burden foisted upon him by an interfering state ('That should keep the fire department happy for another six months'). A fictionalised caricature of an eccentric hotel owner Cleese encountered during his stay at a Torquay hotel in 1970, Basil loses his patience with his guests who wait for the drill in the lobby after confusing the sound of the safe's alarm with the fire alarm, declaring, 'I don't know why we bother; we should let you all burn.'[3]

Basil was obliged to conduct regular drills of his staff and guests in order to satisfy his legal responsibility as a hotelier. Under the 1971 Fire Precautions Act, Basil and his real-life counterparts were to ensure adequate means of

---

[1] Rama Mäkhä, 'Basil Fawlty as a "Pre-Thatcherite" Conservative in Fawlty Towers', *Journal of European Popular Culture* 8, no. 2 (2017): 109–23.

[2] John Cleese and Connie Booth, 'The Germans', *Fawlty Towers*, Series 1, Episode 6 (BBC, first broadcast 24 October 1975).

[3] Cleese and Booth, 'The Germans'.

escape were provided; exits well lit by emergency lighting and unobstructed; smoke alarms properly installed; staff trained in fire drill; and that any proposed changes to the layout or use of the property did not interfere with safe egress.[4] As a proprietors' guide put it bluntly:

> Fire in this hotel could spell DISASTER ... Injury to your colleagues, to our guests. Perhaps even death. Damage to the building, to furniture and equipment. Partial or even total destruction of the hotel. A 'closed for business' notice on the front door. Loss of trade. Loss of jobs.[5]

Fire safety experts insisted that bedroom doors should be self-closing to reduce the risk of fire spread and the number of casualties at night. In fact, an adult was ten times more likely to be caught in a fire at a hotel than at home, even if the risk of death was roughly equal.[6] A fire authority could therefore use the threat of withholding its award of certification to compel a proprietor to make improvements to the safety of the premises.

The mocking of the fire drill in 'The Germans' is revealing of contradictory cultural attitudes towards fire safety at the time. Whereas Basil fails to grasp the seriousness of the fire drill and of maintaining precautionary equipment, his staff (with the exception of Manuel) are well trained in the use of extinguishers, and his guests are prepared to briefly interrupt their holidays to participate in the drill. As an everyday occurrence that takes place in hotels, shops, offices and other workplaces across the country, the fire drill has been used as a comedic device in situation comedies since the 1970s, which indicates the general lack of seriousness with which it is treated by many people until they experience a serious fire first-hand. Yet the fire drill is now a longstanding practice in hotel management, alongside the provision of other precautions, including clear signage, emergency lighting, self-closing doors, smoke alarms and information notices prominently displayed in rooms and public spaces. Together, these micro instances of state regulation shape our movement around a building in small but significant ways and bring familiarity to our experience when staying away from home for work or leisure. While the costs of installation and maintenance could be expensive for small guesthouses, and regarded by some (real and fictional) proprietors and politicians as burdensome regulation, these everyday precautions were integral for the protection of guests and staff following a number of multiple-fatality fires in hotels during the 1960s

---

[4] Home Office, *Guide to the Fire Precautions Act 1971. 1 Hotels and Boarding Houses* (London: HMSO, 1972).

[5] *Act Quickly! Seconds Count!* (London: Hotel and Catering Industry Board, 1984).

[6] S.E. Chandler, 'Fires in Hotels', *Fire Research Note* (London: HMSO, 1969).

and early 1970s. New laws introduced powers of inspection, certification and enforcement by local fire authorities in order to reduce the risk of mass-casualty fires in hotels and similar establishments and, as we shall see, were successful in this aim.

This chapter will examine the context surrounding the introduction of the Fire Precautions Act in 1971 and its impact in reducing the risk to life in hotels. It shows the growing significance of fire prevention to the practice of everyday life and reveals the importance of acting upon the lessons learned from mass-casualty fires in such premises. It also, following on from the previous chapter, traces the emerging anti-regulatory landscape within British government from the mid-1970s, which included resisting proposals to extend the law on fire precautions to other sectors, including old people's homes and hospitals, following multiple-fatality fires. A neoliberal approach towards fire precautions, which increasingly placed responsibility for health and safety on the individual rather than the state, gained momentum during the 1970s and intensified from the 1980s. Ministers regarded fire precautions, like building regulations, as 'burdens on business'. Evidence presented to the Grenfell Tower Inquiry repeatedly cites government ministers' warnings to 'not increase the burden of regulation', even following devastating fires such as that at Lakanal House in 2009.[7] The Conservative-Liberal Democrat Coalition Government (2010–15) even operated a Red Tape Challenge, co-ordinated by the Cabinet Office, which was welcomed by ministers as simulating a competitive game to reduce red tape on the grounds that, to quote the former permanent secretary of the department for local government, 'regulation was not seen as something valuable, it was seen as something that created costs and burdens'.[8]

As we shall see, gaming the regulatory system cost lives. A precautionary approach towards safety was shaped and constrained by the continued occurrence of multiple-fatality fires from the late 1960s through to the 1980s and beyond. This resulted in the law on fire precautions being modified on several occasions in order to extend cover to sporting stadiums and public transport premises during the 1980s. As Majone has argued, the growing impetus towards the deregulation of public services in the 1980s and 1990s led in actuality to 'less restrictive or rigid regulation, rather than no regulation'.[9] The subsequent decision taken by the New Labour Government to reform

[7] See, eg, GTI, BSR00000095/50, Michael Mansfield QC et al., 'Module 6 Opening Submissions: Central Government and Testing & Certification. On Behalf of the Bereaved, Survivors and Residents Represented by Team 2', 19 November 2021, 11.

[8] GTI, Testimony of Dame Melanie Dawes, 16 March 2022, 229.

[9] Majone, 'Paradoxes', 53.

the law in 2005, by introducing the 'responsible person' for managing fire safety while simultaneously limiting the powers of fire authorities to enforce compliance, marked the culmination of the deregulation of fire safety started during the 1980s. Failures of regulatory oversight in growing numbers and varieties of multi-occupancy buildings can thus be traced back to decisions taken to fragment the state's responsibility for fire safety, as well as a lack of political will to extend the law on fire precautions in the aftermath of multiple-fatality fires during the present century.

The beginnings of proactive regulation

A fire precautions act capable of regulating multiple social and economic risks was first mooted in 1962 when the Home Office established an inter-departmental committee 'to consider the principles on which fire prevention legislation should be based and the objects to which it should be directed'. Its report, issued at the end of the year, criticised the inflexibility of existing legislation, which managed risks on a narrow sectoral basis.[10] Legislation, recently passed, affected factories and licensed premises, while officials had drafted similar legislation governing offices, shops and railway premises. Each site was inspected by the fire brigade and a certificate issued, which contained details, marked on approved plans, of the available means of escape and the number of persons allowed on the premises at any given time. Such legislation responded to multiple-fatality fires in industrial workplaces (for example, at a Keighley mill in 1956, in which eight workers died), department stores (with prominent fires in Glasgow and Liverpool high street stores in 1949 and 1960, causing thirteen and eleven deaths, respectively) and places of public amusement (as with a Bolton nightclub fire in 1961, with nineteen deaths). These fatalities temporarily brought the issues to the forefront of the political agenda because of the media interest they generated, but they soon faded from memory.[11]

A consolidatory bill was promoted – and withdrawn due to lack of parliamentary time – on three occasions during the 1960s. Eventually, in 1971 it reached the statute books with cross-party support. Officially, governments were awaiting the publication of the report of the Departmental Committee on the Fire Service, which had been appointed in 1967 to inquire into the organisation of the service. When that finally appeared in May 1970,

---

[10] TNA HO/346/98, 'Fire Prevention Legislation: Memorandum', January 1965.
[11] Shane Ewen, *Fighting Fires: Creating the British Fire Service, c.1800–1978* (Basingstoke: Palgrave, 2010), 157–8.

the idea of consolidating existing fire prevention legislation into a single comprehensive act was rejected.[12]

In truth, the legislation had already been drafted and governments were playing for time, rarely regarding fire safety as a priority. The decision to begin with hotels was again a response to several multiple-fatality fires in the sector in the late 1960s and the result of joint pressure from government advisers and industry bodies to better protect the safety of staff and guests. This included a fire at a hotel in Stornoway, on the Outer Hebrides, a chain of islands off the west coast of mainland Scotland, in 1966, caused by a carelessly discarded cigarette. The hotel's outdated alarm system consisted of a bell which was not audible throughout the whole premises; five guests lost their lives. A further five fatalities occurred at a fire in a hotel in Church Stretton, Shropshire in 1968, where bedroom notices advised guests: 'In case of fire shout "FIRE"'. A third fire at the Rose & Crown coaching inn in Saffron Walden, Essex, on Boxing Day in 1969 caused eleven deaths when a faulty television set caught alight overnight. All three fires occurred in old buildings, with combustible timber floors and staircases, which blocked escape and access points. Experts estimated that the average age of hotels was between 50 and 100 years, with some coaching inns over 200 years old, built before modern regulations were introduced, but full of historic charm. The Rose & Crown, for instance, was a sixteenth-century coaching inn with 'old-world atmosphere', but, lacking suitable precautions, firefighters found that fire-resisting doors failed during Christmas festivities.[13]

Shortly before the fire at the Rose & Crown, the Fire Protection Association (FPA), an industry body formed in 1946 by fire insurance companies, issued a stark warning about inadequate precautions in hotels, citing failings with the construction, equipment and training of staff in many of the estimated 200,000 premises across Britain. The British Hotels and Restaurants Association, a lobby group for the hospitality industry, dismissed the report as 'unnecessarily alarmist', but the number of fire disasters disproved its weak argument.[14] That so few hotels contained up-to-date fire precautions was ridiculed by *Fire* magazine, which mocked up a fake advertisement for a hotel offering 'Bed, Breakfast and Fire Risk' for its readers, who were well versed in the use of gallows humour to cope with the grim realities of the profession:

[12] TNA HO/346/97-99; *Report of the Departmental Committee on the Fire Service*, Cmd. 4371 (London: HMSO, 1970), 163–4.

[13] *The Times*, 3 April 1968, 1; *Daily Mirror*, 27 December 1969, 1–2.

[14] *Fire Protection Association Journal*, 83 (1969), 325–31.

HOTEL, facing beach. Excellent cuisine. All mod. con., comfortable beds. Children welcome. Highly combustible. Unenclosed staircases, limited means of escape.[15]

To remind Parliament of the importance of legislating change, a fire, causing the deaths of eight guests, occurred at the New Langham hotel in London in May 1971. Moving the second reading of the Fire Precautions Bill, Minister of State Richard Sharples argued that it was 'a fact that all too often in the past before action has been taken, it has needed some major catastrophe to focus attention' on lawmakers; the new bill offered the chance to deal proactively with hazards as they appeared or evolved.[16]

The bill, then, was based on years of applied learning but it took the trigger of the Rose & Crown blaze – cited by both Judith Hackitt and Sam Webb as a 'milestone event' in regulatory reform[17] – to overcome delays with its drafting. An internal inquiry by Chief Inspector of Fire Services Henry Smith revealed multiple defects in the hotel and criticised the owners, Trust House Hotels, for failing to invite the local brigade to make a goodwill inspection of the premises. Given that Trust House Ltd. was in the process of merging with Forte Holdings to create the country's largest hotel group, Smith recognised the urgency to impose a clear duty upon 'hotel managements in ensuring that fire precautions are strictly observed', as well as upon staff and guests in 'avoiding thoughtless actions such as the failure to extinguish smoking materials properly or to close fire and smoke doors on landings or in passages'.[18] What had once been deemed acceptable risks within the hotel industry – not least permitting smoking in bedrooms as well as public areas – had given way to a view that guest and staff safety was as much a priority as the provision of amenities for comfort.

Towards a fire service-led approach

Despite cross-sectoral support, the 1972 Designation Order attracted fierce criticism from hoteliers, trade bodies and Tory MPs that too many fire prevention officers (FPOs) were inflexible in their interpretation of the law, which is certainly hinted at in Basil Fawlty's protest at having to hold a fire drill to satisfy the local brigade. Robert Adley, a Dorset MP and industry

[15] *Fire*, June 1974, 7.

[16] Quoted in *Firefighter*, November/December 1970, 1.

[17] Hackitt, *Interim Report*, 31–2; GTI, SWE00000001/30, Witness Statement, Sam Webb, 8 July 2022, 30.

[18] TNA HO/346/97, 'Fire at Rose and Crown Hotel, Saffron Walden', 29 December 1969; *Report of Her Majesty's Chief Inspector of Fire Services for the Year 1969*, Cmd. 4397 (London: HMSO, 1970), 11.

lobbyist (he was European marketing director for Commonwealth Holiday Inns), bemoaned the 'too tough firemen' whose overzealous attitudes towards safety were 'cutting away at the grass roots of the industry' by 'hitting very hard' small hotels struggling to fund expensive and unnecessary improvements. One such 'small hotel' of twenty-one bedrooms, owned by Exeter MP John Hannam, had been sent an 'improvement notice' containing works totalling £8,000. Meanwhile, an editorial in the *Caterer and Hotelkeeper* magazine dismissed the regulations as 'administratively mad' and 'fiscally stupid'.[19] Complaints were twofold: first, that modern hotels were built to agreed international standards of safety that minimised the risk of fire; second, that the costs of modifying small hotels outweighed the risks as well as the benefits of keeping them open, but legislators had already recognised this by exempting premises that catered for fewer than six guests. Sir Fitzroy Maclean, MP for Bute and Northern Ayrshire who co-owned the historic Creggans Inn on the idyllic shore of Loch Fyne, claimed that the cost of updating safety in historic premises threatened to drive 'run-of-the-mill' hotels such as his out of business. More seriously, historian John Walton notes that many landladies in seaside resorts like Blackpool converted their guesthouses into flatlets partly to avoid the cost of installing fire precautions, as well as in response to the changing pattern of demand from tourists; this would return to haunt them a decade later, as we shall see in Chapter 4.[20]

Multiple-fatality fires in hotels continued to occur, then, in the face of resistance to change. In April 1972, two women died in a fire that destroyed a 1920s Cambridge hotel with no audible alarm system; its management had failed to act on a list of requirements identified during a recent inspection.[21] In July 1973, ten holidaymakers were killed in a devastating fire at the Esplanade Hotel in the Scottish resort town of Oban, started by a carelessly discarded cigarette. A fire brigade inspection the previous year had recommended improvements including smoke-stopping doors and an external escape. The hotel owner was aware of the risks but had postponed the remedial work because of a combination of costs and time, citing the excuse, 'I just didn't get round to it.' Neither had he bothered to train his seasonal staff in fire evacuation because '[t]hey were here for six months only and were mostly girls'.[22] In their coverage of the fire, newspapers

[19] *Fire*, July 1974, 72; Hansard (Commons), 17 December 1974, 1503–41.
[20] Hansard (Commons), 20 February 1973, 429–30; John Walton, *The Blackpool Landlady: A Social History* (Manchester: Manchester University Press, 1978), 198–9.
[21] *Daily Mail*, 25 April 1972, 9.
[22] *Daily Mail*, 25 July 1973, 1, 16.

demanded unsafe hotels be forced to close until they completed approved work, while industry groups and Tory MPs called upon government to offer low-interest loans to support remedial work.[23] As many as half of Britain's hotels and boarding houses could be 'potential death traps' according to an investigation by the *Daily Mirror*, which claimed that up to a quarter of all proprietors flouted the law by not applying for safety certificates. Even then, fire brigades faced a considerable backlog in inspecting and reinspecting premises: in Blackpool, for instance, only 10 per cent of the 4,000 applications for certificates submitted to the local brigade had been completed by mid-1973.[24]

The main problem with the application of the Act, then, concerned workload and resourcing, particularly in tourist areas with a denser concentration of hotels. On the eve of the Act, there were 1,248 full-time FPOs in post, performing between them some 650,000 surveys and inspections nationally. Duties ranged from routine surveys to on-site inspections, which varied from a few minutes for a low-risk premises like a public toilet to three days for large risks such as hospitals; a hotel survey could take anywhere between half a day and a full day, absorbing more person-hours per inspection than most other types of visit.[25]

Civil servants calculated that, even with a phased introduction of the Act, it would still take a decade to extend to 442,000 'high-risk' premises. In the short term, this would involve inspecting and certifying approximately 30,000 hotels and boarding houses. To do so, the fire service would require 350 additional staff, whose role would be limited to fire prevention work. At a modest annual cost of approximately £1 million (equivalent to £14 million in 2020) falling onto the taxpayer, the proposals were fiercely resisted by some local authority associations but welcomed by the Fire Brigades Union (FBU) and Trades Union Congress, which favoured the greater opportunities for career advancement that the Act promised firefighters.[26]

Implementation was inevitably piecemeal, but not without success. By the close of 1974, fire authorities across England and Wales had issued certificates for 3,302 hotels and boarding houses. A further 13,202 premises had been issued with improvement notices, while 24,985 were awaiting inspection.

[23] Hansard (Lords), 25 February 1975, 644.

[24] *Daily Mirror*, 25 July 1973, 1–2.

[25] *Report of Her Majesty's Chief Inspector of Fire Services for the Year 1970*, Cmd. 4700 (London: HMSO, 1971), 12.

[26] TNA HO/346/98, 'Note on the Implementation of the Bill', undated, 9; *Firefighter*, October 1971, 1.

An estimated 14,000 premises had yet to submit applications. Three years later, 20,000 premises had been certified, with 10,000 more outstanding applications or appeals in the system. Progress was slow but welcomed by many in the service, not least Chief Inspector of Fire Services Kenneth Holland, who, in addressing industry management in his annual reports, stressed that fire precautions 'are an investment in keeping a business going'.[27] Despite the backlog, a survey by the FPA in 1978 concluded that the number of hotel fires involving fatalities had fallen significantly in the six years since the Order's designation.[28] According to government data, proactive regulation was proven to save lives. In 1974 there were thirty-one deaths and eighty-one non-fatal casualties in hotel fires in Britain; six years later, nineteen fatalities were recorded in hotels, hostels and boarding houses (of which ten were accounted for in a single blaze at a London hostel – see Chapter 4) and one hundred and thirty-nine casualties. There was now a greater proportion of fire-related deaths in unregulated premises such as homes, nightclubs, public houses and restaurants.[29] Casualty rates in hotels and boarding houses continued to fall during the 1980s, despite the number of fires remaining fairly constant.[30] Inspection, certification and enforcement had been proven to succeed in raising awareness among staff and guests as well as in improving hotel management and housekeeping. By the end of the 1970s, consumer groups had even declared British hotels to be safer than many of their European counterparts and the Fire Precautions Act was adopted as a model of good practice by other countries.[31]

The deregulatory impulse

The success of the 1972 Designation Order in raising standards of safety within hotels inevitably led to calls from stakeholder groups to extend its provisions to undesignated sectors. Successive home secretaries faced pressure to issue designation orders governing public sector premises including psychiatric

[27] *Report of Her Majesty's Chief Inspector of Fire Services for the Year 1973*, Cmd. 5674 (London: HMSO, 1974), 34; A.R. Everton and Gordon Cooke, 'The Legislation', in Jane Taylor and Gordon Cooke, eds., *The Fire Precautions Act in Practice* (London: Architectural Press, 1978), 28.

[28] Fire Protection Association, 'Fire Problems in Hotels', in Taylor and Cooke, *Fire Precautions*, 29.

[29] Department of the Environment and Fire Offices' Committee, *UK Fire Statistics* (London: HMSO, 1975), 24–5; Home Office, *Fire Statistics United Kingdom* (London: HMSO, 1981), 19.

[30] The number of fires in the sector fluctuated between 1,600 and 1,800 from 1972 to 1987 and rose to 2,000 in 1988; see *UK Fire Statistics*, 1972–88.

[31] Holiday Which?, *Fire in Hotels: An Investigation* (London: Consumers' Association, 1979).

hospitals, nursing homes, hostels, student halls of residence, schools and high-rise residential buildings.[32] Reformist voices grew louder in the wake of disasters in institutions where 'at-risk' people were cared for, not least because they frequently exposed underlying stigma towards vulnerable groups. First, in July 1972 a devastating fire at the Coldharbour Hospital in Dorset, used as a home for people with learning disabilities, killed thirty residents. The committee of inquiry's investigation found understaffing, while serious safety defects were discovered following a renovation. When the contractors proposed to use fire-resistant plasterboard partitions in wards, they were advised against this by the consulting architect on the grounds that plasterboard 'might be vulnerable to kicking and other behaviour from the patients'; subsequently, contractors installed a more flammable hardboard which gave it the highest fire risk rating possible.[33]

Such derogatory remarks reveal the prevalence of prejudice in cases where some of the most disadvantaged people who demand improvements in building safety are stigmatised either as 'troublemakers' – as was the case with several residents of Grenfell Tower in the months and years leading up to the fire – or as undeserving of the extra expense.[34] Yet the government shied away from challenging such blatant instances of 'stigma power', with its social services secretary, Keith Joseph, describing the calamitous decision to use hessian to cover hardboard partitions as 'misguided enthusiasm' before committing his government to strengthening the enforcing powers of fire authorities. In truth, little changed and Joseph warned that '[w]ith the best will in the world it is not possible to guarantee that such appalling accidents as that at Coldharbour will never occur again'.[35]

Two years later, in December 1974, eighteen residents, aged between sixty-seven and ninety-one years, died in a fire at an old people's home in Nottinghamshire caused by a resident smoking in bed. Staff shortages were again cited as a failure in evacuating those residents with physical impairments. The home, a prefabricated single-storey building comprising houses connected to a dining hall, was designed by the architect Donald Gibson and was part of the Consortium of Local Authorities Programme

---

[32] Fire Brigades Union, *Grenfell Tower Fire*, 12–13.

[33] *Report of the Committee of Inquiry into the Fire at Coldharbour Hospital, Sherborne on 5 July 1972*, Cmd. 5170, 8–9, 41–2.

[34] GTI, IWS00002109/1, Second Witness Statement of Edward Daffarn, 6 May 2020, 2–3.

[35] *Daily Telegraph*, 11 January 1973, 19; TNA CAB/129/166/28, Keith Joseph, 'Report on the Fire at Coldharbour Hospital', 12 December 1972; Tracy Shildrick, 'Lessons from Grenfell: Poverty Propaganda, Stigma and Class Power', *The Sociological Review Monographs* 66, no. 4 (2018): 783–98.

(CLASP) system of industrialised building. Initially bringing together local authorities to meet the problem of building schools on land subject to mining subsidence, using bulk purchasing methods as well as on-site assembly of factory-made parts, CLASP was used to construct residential accommodation, hospitals and universities during the 1960s.[36]

Concerns were repeatedly raised about the safety of such buildings, specifically in their use of false ceilings, which created a flue with the wooden and felt roofs, and a spate of fires in CLASP schools during the 1970s caused experts to dismiss the system as unsafe.[37] Although a 1971 amendment to the Building Regulations included a stipulation that fireproof partitions should be inserted behind ceiling panels, fire investigators found that remediation work had yet to begin. Following a campaign by the National Corporation for the Care of Old People, the newly elected Labour Government promised to extend regulations to residential homes. Draft regulations were drawn up to strengthen precautions, but because of a change in government in 1979 these were never issued.[38]

The failure to extend the provisions of the 1971 Act to protect 'at-risk' groups reveals a hardening attitude within government towards the value of regulation. It also reflects a preference for individuals to take greater responsibility for themselves regardless of whether they are able to do so and assumes that people will behave rationally or with urgency in an emergency, which is not guaranteed, as several empirical studies have shown.[39] While advisory bodies attempted to shape a more proactive approach to policymaking, ministers largely interpreted their responsibility for protecting public safety as an administrative and financial exercise rather than a moral one. As we saw in the previous chapter, this is a view that has been recently reinforced by the government's decision not to implement the recommendation in the Grenfell Tower Inquiry Phase I Report that all disabled residents be given Personal Emergency Evacuation Plans (PEEPs) on the grounds that their costs would be disproportionate to the number of lives likely to be saved.

The limitations to the regulatory approach should be understood in the context of an escalating economic crisis during the 1970s, as well as

---

[36] *Report of the Committee of Inquiry into the Fire at Fairfield Home, Edwalton, Nottinghamshire, on 15 December 1974*, Cmd. 6149, July 1975; TNA MH/160/1047-8, Committee of Inquiry; Andrew Saint, *Towards a Social Architecture: The Role of School Building in Post-War England* (New Haven, CT: Yale University Press, 1987).

[37] *Daily Mail*, 17 December 1974, 11.

[38] TNA MH/154/834, 'Fire Precautions in Old People's Homes'; *Report of Her Majesty's Chief Inspector of Fire Services for the Year 1978*, Cmd. 7605, 22.

[39] David Canter, ed., *Fires and Human Behaviour*, 2nd edition (London: Fulton, 1990).

growing distrust of local authorities from within central government.[40] Labour ministers regularly cited public expenditure restrictions as obstacles to enforcement, while industry bodies resisted proposals to extend regulatory provisions to the hospitality sector, citing a large proportion of its membership 'struggling for survival in the face of the present economic depression'.[41] Successive governments were therefore committed to permitting a greater degree of self-compliance within business in assessing their own workplace hazards free from state restrictions.

The influence of neoliberal ideas over the limits of the regulatory state became more strident from 1979 with the election of a Conservative government openly committed to diminishing the role of the state, cutting public expenditure, slashing regulations, curbing trade union powers and restricting interference in individual enterprise. The model of inspection and certification established by the Fire Precautions Act was regarded as out of kilter with the Thatcher Government's embrace of a 'neoliberal revolution'.[42] Yet the continued occurrence of fires – including one at an old people's home outside Hull, which killed six residents and injured another twenty-one in 1977 – amplified warnings for stricter regulation of care homes.[43] Although Labour's draft regulations designating residential accommodation were at an advanced stage of preparation by April 1979, they attracted considerable resistance from within the care sector. In particular, concerns about inflexibility and costs of compliance were raised by the Personal Social Services Council (PSSC), a non-governmental advisory body established in 1971. The PSSC issued a report arguing that 'the quality of life in residential homes suffers as a result of fire precautions', citing difficulties caused to resident mobility by self-closing doors as well as the likely impact of the costs of remedial work resulting in 'a cut-back' in care. Rather than a one-size-fits-all certification process, the PSSC recommended a compromise approach 'more carefully tailored to the needs of individual homes'.[44]

Seizing on the criticism, the reforms were put on hold with the Conservative's election victory before the PSSC was itself disbanded following public spending cuts.[45] Moreover, rather than advocating a

---

[40] Jim Tomlinson, *The Politics of Decline: Understanding Post-War Britain* (London: Routledge, 2001).

[41] Hansard (Commons), 27 November 1975, 1035.

[42] Jeremy Green, 'Anglo-American Development, the Euromarkets, and the Deeper Origins of Neoliberal Deregulation', *Review of International Studies* 42 (2016): 443.

[43] Hansard (Commons), 14 January 1977, 603–4.

[44] Diana Seabright, *Fire and Care: An Enquiry into Fire Precautions in Residential Homes* (London: Personal Social Services Council, 1979).

[45] TNA MH/154/834, 28 April 1979, 15 June 1981.

flexible approach towards fire precautions, the new government tightened restrictions on expenditure, which compelled local authorities to make cuts to social care and firefighting.[46] Mandatory fire precautions were viewed suspiciously by ministers who preferred to issue advisory guidance to service providers rather than insist upon 'excessive expenditure' and 'stringent requirements' at a time of 'scarce public, private and charitable funds'.[47] As Home Secretary Leon Brittan put it in response to a Commons motion about care homes, 'In many cases in both public and private sectors there is no doubt that steps have already been taken to achieve an acceptable standard of fire precautions' without resorting to enforcement. 'This is what is desired, whether it is done by certification or without certification.' The Home Office thus rejected proposals from its own advisory body, the Central Fire Brigades Advisory Council (CFBAC), to phase in the designation of old people's homes, preferring to encourage care providers to take advantage of the available voluntary guidance.[48]

Politicians and civil servants repeatedly cited the Fire Precautions Act as an example of excessive regulation in a political atmosphere that was keen to redefine the boundaries between the public and private sectors. In 1980, the Home Office published a green paper criticising both the escalating costs of enforcing the legislation (at approximately £16.25 million a year) and the costs of compliance for designated premises, which it estimated at about £70 million per year. Stopping short of recommending the dismantling of the existing regulatory framework, the authors proposed 'a modified system', awarding powers to fire authorities to selectively focus on class A risks (premises in larger industrial and commercial cities) rather than 'premises presenting a low risk'.[49] Greater flexibility resonates with what Michael Moran calls the 'hyper-innovative approach' towards the operation of the British regulatory state that emerged from the late 1970s, as a response by the British political system to a policy crisis that eroded confidence in the post-war social and political consensus as well as a crisis of belief in the ability of government to govern in an accountable fashion. The 'new regulatory state' that emerged involved standardising and formalising the practices of government through the provision of systematic information and uniform reporting and control mechanisms.[50] In relation to fire precautions,

[46] Hansard (Lords), 24 October 1979, 91–2.
[47] Hansard (Commons), 28 January 1980, 1094.
[48] Hansard (Commons), 28 January 1980, 1096.
[49] Home Office, *Future Fire Policy: A Consultative Document* (London: HMSO, 1980), 7, 27–8.
[50] Moran, *British Regulatory State*, 6–7.

government thus accepted its general duty to provide a reasonable standard of safety towards property and human life, but left it to others – not least the fire protection industry and fire brigades – to establish what this meant in practice. Whereas the Fire Precautions Act had ushered in a new era of standardised control within government, this discernible shift towards greater selectivity was designed to disrupt and disperse its own regulatory powers while enabling more independent enterprise.

In 1985, a second review of fire precautions advocated even greater selectivity in the law's application. While this was influenced by the growing number of European Council directives concerning health and safety, which extended the principle of employer self-compliance beyond the limits permitted under British legislation, it was ostensibly driven by central government's crusade against 'burdens on business', as explored in the previous chapter.[51] The deregulation of administrative and legislative regulations imposed upon business had emerged as a flagship element in British government policy by the mid-1980s and was part of a wider transnational deregulatory moment in Western societies; the state was committed to 'rolling back' on its micro-management of the economy through a variety of methods including privatising public utilities and cutting 'red tape', as business regulations were derogatorily described by ministers. Fire precautions were identified as one of the most 'complicated' and inconsistently applied requirements for firms to adhere to in Lord Young's *Burdens of Business* report, published in the same year. 'Fire precautions should be made more flexible for premises with a minimal fire risk', argued Young, recommending 'a new system of control' with greater flexibility in order to avoid 'unnecessarily severe requirements on low risk premises but consistently catching and improving high risk premises'.[52]

In their jointly authored foreword to the Home Office's review, Leon Britten and Lord Young cited the recent fire at Bradford City Football Club's Valley Parade Stadium, which fatally injured fifty-six supporters in 'horrific scenes' that 'brought home to everyone the devastating effects of fire and the need for adequate fire precautions'.[53] What they failed to mention was the fact that years of flammable waste – old newspapers, cigarette packets, polystyrene cups and other discarded items were found by forensic investigators – had been allowed to accumulate underneath the wooden stand, which provided fuel for a discarded light (either a dropped match or a cigarette) when it

---

[51] Home Office, *A Review of the Fire Precautions Act 1971: A Consultative Document* (London: HMSO, 1985).

[52] *Lifting the Burden*, 27–8.

[53] Home Office, *A Review of the Fire Precautions Act 1971*, foreword.

fell through the gaps in the dilapidated stand. Left to smoulder under the feet of spectators gathered to celebrate the club's championship winning season, once alight the fire quickly spread up the embankment and ignited the pitch roof, causing a flashover that cut off escape for many and led to one survivor describing the fire's ferocious spread as 'Four Minutes to Hell'. The club chairman's decision to remove fire extinguishers from stands, on the spurious grounds that they would be misused by spectators, further reveals the ways that regulatory failures can quickly escalate, in this instance by delaying assistance from arriving. The government's review, reinforced by the accompanying public inquiry, therefore used the opportunity to censure the club owners' failure towards their supporters, while introducing stricter safety rules for sporting stadiums, thereby introducing a necessary regulatory 'burden' to protect public safety.[54]

The resultant Fire Safety and Safety of Places of Sport Act 1987 required fire authorities to take an interventionist approach in certifying outdoor stadiums as well as indoor sporting premises. To offset the increased workload this entailed, the 1971 Act was amended, granting local authorities powers to exempt low-risk premises from certification. This hierarchy of risks was further refined following the devastating fire at London King's Cross Underground Station in November 1987, which killed thirty-one people including London Fire Brigade station officer Colin Townsley. As a result, sub-surface railway stations were designated as class A risks following the relaxation of rules for low-risk premises. 'This is the speediest means to introduce enforceable standards without uncertainty', claimed Home Secretary Douglas Hurd, recognising that there were occasions when 'the regulatory system can evolve' in order to deal with new or emerging risks.[55]

'Rolling back the state' and deregulation continued as twin pillars of government policy into the 1990s and beyond and, in the relative absence of high-profile fires, they met with greater success. Michael Heseltine's Deregulation and Contracting Out Bill in 1994 clumsily promised 'the biggest bonfire of controls that has taken place in modern times in this country', although it failed to deliver the forecasted savings, while, from 1997, New Labour promised to accelerate the removal of 'unnecessarily

[54] Oliver Popplewell, *Committee of Inquiry into Crowd Safety and Control at Sports Grounds: Interim Report*, Cmd. 9585 (London: HMSO, 1985); Paul Firth, *Four Minutes to Hell: The Story of the Bradford City Fire* (Manchester: Parrs Wood Press, 2005); Shane Ewen and Aaron Andrews, 'The Media, Affect, and Community in a Decade of Disasters: Reporting the 1985 Bradford City Stadium Fire', *Contemporary British History* 35, no. 2 (2021): 258–83.
[55] *The Times*, 10 November 1988, 16; Hackitt, *Interim Report*, 32.

burdensome' regulations, with fire precautions identified as 'a priority target' for its Better Regulation Task Force.[56] A variety of voices – in particular newspapers and policy 'think tanks' – spoke out against fire precautions and health and safety rules using negative rhetorical tropes such as 'red tape' and advocated relaxing policy around risk regulation.[57] This coincided with the emergence of a managerialist approach within government, which translated into using deregulation to enable greater private and voluntary sector involvement in the provision of public services through multi-agency partnerships. The state was shifting from a traditional service delivery role to one where it contracted out public services to private or voluntary bodies. Just like public utilities or building control, fire precautions were no longer regarded as natural monopolies of the state but would be passed back to the individual to determine the appropriateness of controls. From 1997, fire risk assessments were introduced into workplaces to satisfy European Commission directives. Two years later, amended regulations set a requirement for premises designated under the 1971 Act to also conduct fire risk assessments; this applied to all workplaces, including hotels, boarding houses and care homes. The duplication of administrative effort strengthened criticism that the European Commission unnecessarily tied British firms up in red tape and reinforced an increasingly hostile media attitude towards 'Brussels bureaucrats'.[58] While this culminated most notoriously with the British government's decision to leave the European Union in 2016, it was also cited by several witnesses at the Grenfell Tower Inquiry as justification for the 'one-in, one-out' strategy for reducing regulations pursued by successive governments during the 2010s.[59]

Eventually and perhaps inevitably, an overhaul of the law came at the turn of the twenty-first century, thereby establishing the regulatory regime under which the fire at Grenfell Tower occurred. From 1997 to 2007, the New Labour Government, with Tony Blair as prime minister, continued the move to deregulate fire precautions while also championing the modernisation of public services. In practice, this meant greater hollowing out of the public sector and a more active role for private enterprise in delivering services. Blair's 'modernisation agenda' was intended to distance 'New' from 'Old' Labour by demonstrating the party's ability to govern after years in opposition. It was justified as a means to de-align the Labour Party

---

[56] *Financial Times*, 7 December 2000, 5.
[57] *Financial Times*, 1 July 1992, 9; Almond and Esbester, 'Legitimate Risks?', 277–8.
[58] Prosser and Taylor, *Grenfell Tower Fire*, 75.
[59] GTI, INQ00014583/1, Department for Communities and Local Government, 'Strategy for Reducing Regulation' (2011), submitted 23 February 2022.

from its traditional supporters, in particular trade unions, and open up public services to a wider variety of influences.[60] The fire service and the law on fire precautions were not immune to this, as seen in the controversial recommendations made by an independent review chaired by the university administrator George Bain in 2002 and a white paper issued the following year. Deaths and injuries from fire had declined during the second half of the 1990s, yet the number of fires had risen since 1998, which led the review to recommend the service take a risk-based approach towards safety, focusing on the 'most vulnerable' people in society – lower socio-economic groups, single-parent households, people with disabilities, the elderly, renters in houses in multiple occupancy (HMOs) and households with heavy smokers and/or drinkers – who suffered disproportionately from fire and its effects. Bain contended that the fire service's advisory bodies were resistant to modernisation and overly focused on 'stakeholder business to the detriment of progressing national strategic issues', reportedly blocking reforms.[61] The Home Office had, according to some insiders, actively treated the fire service with 'benign neglect' compared to its core matters of crime and immigration. New Labour transferred responsibility for fire service policy to the Department for Transport, Local Government and the Regions in 2001 and, from 2002, to the Office of the Deputy Prime Minister (ODPM), believing that 'new sets of eyes' would bring 'new perspectives' and help to elevate the service's low status within government.[62]

The Bain Review exacerbated deteriorating industrial relations within the service, witnessed in a national firefighters' strike in 2002 and the FBU's disaffiliation from the Labour Party in 2004. Unperturbed by criticism of its 'lack of vision and … contempt of Britain's Fire Service', the ODPM, headed by John Prescott, a former official in the National Union of Seamen, pushed ahead with radical reforms to the service, introduced in 2004 and 2005.[63] As minister for local government, Nick Raynsford, described it, 'The Bain Report was a clarion call for reform in a service that had been left in a time warp, approaching its duties and conducting its industrial relations in ways that smacked of the attitudes of a bygone era.'[64] Much historic

---

[60] Alan Finlayson, *Making Sense of New Labour* (London: Lawrence & Wishart, 2003).

[61] The Independent Review of the Fire Service, *The Future of the Fire Service: Reducing Risk, Saving Lives* (London: Office of the Deputy Prime Minister, 2002), 12–15, 36, 46; Office of the Deputy Prime Minister, *Our Fire and Rescue Service*, Cmd. 5808 (London: HMSO, 2003).

[62] Nick Raynsford, *Substance Not Spin: An Insider's View of Success and Failure in Government* (Bristol: Policy Press, 2016), 145–6, 151.

[63] *Fire*, December 2002, 7.

[64] Raynsford, *Substance*, 153.

legislation was rescinded, abandoning national standards of fire cover introduced after the Second World War in favour of local Integrated Risk Management Plans, reducing limits on the number of operational firefighters required to crew appliances and rashly abolishing its own policy advisory body, the CFBAC. Less contentious was the logical decision to rename the service the Fire and Rescue Service to reflect firefighters' increasing role in non-fire emergency work, which included responding to terrorism, flooding, chemical spillages and road traffic collisions, though successive governments have since shown unwillingness to properly fund these new responsibilities.[65]

The 2005 Regulatory Reform (Fire Safety) Order repealed over seventy separate pieces of legislation including the Fire Precautions Act, introducing a single fire safety regime that applied to all workplaces and non-domestic premises from 2006 in England, Wales and Scotland (from 2010 in Northern Ireland). It also covered premises where the main use is to provide sleeping accommodation, such as hotels, boarding houses, hostels, holiday accommodation and the common areas of higher-risk residential buildings (HRRBs) and HMOs. The Order requires every premises to employ a 'responsible person' to undertake a fire risk assessment (FRA) and decide how to address the risks. It thus signalled a move from a prescriptive regime to a risk-assessment-based approach, removing the responsibility for certification from fire and rescue authorities. This led some commentators to question whether the changes were being driven more by 'economic factors than a need to maintain the current levels of public and employee safety from fire beyond their homes'.[66]

In the years that followed, the number of FRAs undertaken by operational staff fell considerably and fire authorities cut the numbers of fire prevention officers until the Grenfell Tower fire triggered a reversal in the policy. Decades of accumulated knowledge of building risks by operational crews had been degraded; the era of regulation by the fire service had ended. The ODPM issued eleven guidance documents containing practical advice for 'responsible persons' about how to comply with the legislation, although a 2006 poll found that 35 per cent of businesses in England and Wales were unaware of how the legal changes affected them while almost half of respondents were uncertain as to whether they even complied.[67] Given the relatively low level of compliance, experts were sceptical of the benefits of the

[65] Raynsford, *Substance*, 152–6.
[66] *Fire*, March 2005, 19.
[67] *Financial Times*, 10 June 2006, 20.

change to public safety, especially given the existence of 'a vocal minority' of businesses 'who will do absolutely nothing at all unless threatened with legal action'.[68] As Philip Heath, the technical manager for Kingspan Insulation Limited – the firm that provided rainscreen boards used in the refurbishment of Grenfell Tower, which were catastrophically revealed to be combustible – described it in an early assessment of the order's effectiveness at dealing with building insulation products and cladding, '[l]ack of understanding about any material's true performance in a fire situation could at best prove expensive and at worst fatal'.[69] Firefighters and the residents of tower blocks would find out this fact for themselves soon enough, while shocking evidence submitted to the Grenfell Tower Inquiry (in which, after having the safety of the rainscreen cladding questioned by builders, Heath replied in an internal email that they should 'go f*ck themselves') exposed serious defects in the system of self-compliance that successive governments had actively encouraged since the 1980s.[70]

Conclusion

This chapter has traced the shifting attitude and approach of the state towards fire precautions in hotels and other premises. With the exception of the privately owned home, where responsibility for fire safety has been left to the homeowner or landlord, central government begrudgingly accepted its responsibility for regulating fire precautions from 1970. This heel-dragging attitude towards safety manifested itself in a variety of approaches, ranging from reluctant acceptance of the requirement to regulate a greater number and variety of premises during the 1970s to hostility towards the supposed imposition of 'red tape' on private enterprise during the 1980s. Where regulations were rolled out successfully, these were historically reactive to large multiple-fatality fires, which briefly opened policy windows for reform. Scope for more widespread systematic reform was more possible during the Thatcher and Blair years, where there was greater policy continuity across three terms (albeit subject to considerable 'machinery of government' changes). Even then the deregulatory impulses of both governments co-existed alongside the requirement for new regulations that were triggered by crises; in the first instance, by a 'decade of disasters' in the 1980s and, in the second, the firefighters' pay dispute and strike of 2002–3, which presented,

[68] *Fire*, March 2005, 19–20.
[69] *RICS Building Control Journal*, October 2007, 22–3.
[70] *Inside Housing*, 30 November 2020; GTI, Testimony of Philip Heath, 30 November 2020, 122–3.

according to one of the government ministers involved, 'an opportunity' to achieve 'real change' in modernising the service.[71]

Where regulations were properly introduced, they reduced the number of casualties from fire by improving the provision of fire precautions and raising individual and public awareness of safety, as seen most clearly in the case of hotels and boarding houses. Collaboration between the state, industry and service stakeholders, as well as individual proprietors and guests – in familiarising themselves with the location of fire exits, not obstructing corridors and acting promptly when the fire alarm is activated – reduced the number of fatalities in hotel fires between the 1970s and 1990s and independent studies consequently highlighted the relative safety of British hotels compared to their European counterparts. Yet the number and severity of hotel fires rose in England and Wales between 2011 and 2019, with a proportionately greater number of people killed or injured in hotel fires than in flats and apartments over the same period.[72] Even then, the greater life risk has continued to reside in institutional buildings such as hospitals, prisons, hostels and care homes where there are specific challenges with evacuation caused by residents with restricted mobility, cognitive disabilities and other social and medical problems – as has been documented in this chapter.[73]

These worrying facts raise serious questions about the effectiveness of deregulated fire precautions. The inspection and certification of hotels and other public buildings may have been a cumbersome job for under-resourced fire brigades, but it was effective in improving public safety. Moreover, as recent studies have suggested, there are conflicting interpretations over who should be recognised as 'the responsible person' in hotel chains, which has been exposed by the widespread installation of combustible cladding on the frontages of tall buildings across the country. A 2019 cladding fire, fortunately with no fatalities, at the Brentford branch of Travelodge – at which I have stayed while researching for this book – reveals the tension between the deregulatory impulses of the state and micro-level regulatory practices to protect public safety. In his incident report, London Fire Brigade's Assistant Commissioner Graham Ellis reported that the incident

[71] Ewen and Andrews, 'Media', 259–60; Raynsford, *Substance*, 153–4.

[72] *Construction News*, 18 May 2020.

[73] Stuart Hodkinson and Phil Murphy, 'The Fire Risks of Purpose-Built Blocks of Flats: An Exploration of Official Fire Incident Data in England – Interim Research Findings', July 2021, <https://www.bafsa.org.uk/wp-content/uploads/bsk-pdf-manager/2021/07/Fire -Risks-of-Purpose-Built-Blocks-of-Flats-An-exploration-of-Official-Fire-Incident-Data -in-England.pdf>, accessed 7 March 2023.

was 'an excellent example of multi-agencies working together to bring a challenging incident under control with no injuries', yet it also reveals how much we entrust our personal safety to the responsibility of people who put profit above individual safety. As one fire safety expert puts it, 'You know your home and your way around it, but in a hotel, you probably used the lift, and don't even know where the stairs are', which demands extra care to take responsibility for the safety of ourselves and our families.[74]

Far from being stale, the regulatory system established in the 1960s and early 1970s improved safety standards in designated premises and demonstrably saved lives. The failure to extend the law to unregulated sectors was the result of political apathy and instability within successive governments, as well as a conscious effort to deregulate fire precautions from 1979. Political and media interest in matters of safety – which were frequently derided as unwelcome and burdensome within public discourse by right-wing politicians, journalists and fictionalised hotel proprietors alike – only really piqued following high-profile multiple-fatality fires, as has been the case yet again in the wake of the Grenfell tragedy. Local authorities were actively encouraged to avoid a prescriptive approach towards enforcement, using persuasion or administrative sanctions in the majority of cases. The 'paradox of regulation', as Majone describes it, has meant that the deregulation of public services in the 1980s and 1990s involved a cultural shift from a relatively rigid but effective fire service-led approach to a more or less self-regulated regime subject to 'less burdensome methods' such as goodwill safety inspections and the issuing of improvement notices.[75] One can only hope that, to return to our opening example, Basil Fawlty's wife, Sybil, would have taken it upon herself to be 'the responsible person', rather than leave matters to her incompetent husband, otherwise Fawlty Towers would probably have long burned to the ground.

[74] London Fire Brigade, Incident Report, 4 December 2019, <https://www.london-fire .gov.uk/incidents/2019/december/hotel-fire-brentford>; *Construction News*, 18 May 2020, <https://www.constructionnews.co.uk/agenda/hotels-uncovered-the-contractors-locked -in-multi-million-pound-cladding-disputes-18-05-2020/>.
[75] Majone, 'Paradoxes', 53.

3. The mixed economy of 'scientific governance' in twentieth-century Britain

In 1979, a short survey of fires in high-rise buildings in Britain and overseas was published by the Building Research Establishment (BRE), the government's national building research agency. Written by R.E.H. Read, an authority on structural fire safety and a senior officer in the civil service, the survey was commissioned in the wake of multiple high-rise building fires overseas as well as several extraordinary fires in Britain. This included the 1973 fire at the Summerland leisure centre on the Isle of Man, which exposed the unanticipated speed with which cladding fires could take hold of large premises.[1] Summerland was a fine example of the 'cheerful and colourful commercial modernism' of the 1960s and 1970s,[2] but its burning was also a brutal reminder of the construction industry's failure to regulate itself.

While Read concluded that Britain's high-rise buildings did not pose 'a special fire hazard', especially 'when correctly designed and incorporating the right standards', he also identified several defects to guard against. These included the threat of external fire spread through poorly fitted windows or improper compartmentation measures such as unsealed doors and a lack of cavity barriers in ceilings, all of which were demonstrably proven to be catastrophic at Summerland. Read concluded his report with the warning, '[a]s with all types of building, the problems of fire in high-rise situations not only depend upon good design and construction but perhaps to a greater extent on good management'.[3] Poor design, substandard renovations and indifferent management by property developers and housing providers could quickly transform a low-risk scenario into a life-threatening emergency, as revealed by several fires in tower blocks in the following decades, examined later in this chapter, and which prove that the Grenfell Tower fire was a disaster foretold.

---

[1] R.E.H. Read, 'Fire Risks in High-Rise Buildings', *Building Research Establishment Information Paper* (1979), 1.
[2] Otto Saumarez Smith, 'The Lost World of the British Leisure Centre', *History Workshop Journal* 88 (2019): 192.
[3] Read, 'Fire Risks', 1, 3.

Read's report reflected a curiosity among the scientific civil service in advancing their understanding of fire by studying past experiences, thereby strengthening the protection of vulnerable communities. Until its privatisation in 1997, BRE defined its role in terms of the benefit its research accrued for the general public rather than the construction industry. Formed in 1972 through a merger of the government's building and fire research agencies, BRE's roots lay in the development of scientific modes of governance following the First World War. As Don Leggett and Charlotte Sleigh have shown, 'scientific governance' has been taken to refer to both 'the governance *of* science' and 'governance *by* science', with the majority of studies focused on the former's world of professional structures and affiliate institutions.[4] An emerging and important strand within the historiography traces how governments made use of the knowledge of scientific and technocratic experts when making decisions concerning matters of public policy. Historical interest has spanned the fields of national defence, reconstruction planning, healthcare and environmental policy, revealing how the British state has never governed in a vacuum but has drawn upon the expertise and resources of a variety of expert actors – across the public, private, military and voluntary sectors – in advancing the understanding and regulation of science and its benefits throughout the twentieth century, but especially since the end of the Second World War.[5]

BRE and its predecessor institutions pursued a 'mixed-economy' approach towards 'scientific governance', drawing upon existing knowledge and partnerships between public, private and voluntary bodies with an interest in research and its application to daily life. Indeed, joint working across the public and private sectors was at the heart of the governance of fire safety from the early twentieth century and so it could be again with brave policymaking. This chapter, in taking its cue from Sam Wetherell's call for closer examination of the role played by research laboratories in building 'developmental social infrastructure' in twentieth-century Britain, traces the evolution of this 'mixed-economy' approach towards fire research.[6] The earliest phase of scientific testing, originating at the turn of the twentieth

---

[4] Don Leggett and Charlotte Sleigh, 'Scientific Governance: An Introduction', in Leggett and Sleigh, eds., *Scientific Governance in Britain, 1914–79* (Manchester: Manchester University Press, 2016), 2–3.

[5] See, eg, Sabine Clarke, 'Pure Science with a Practical Aim: The Meanings of Fundamental Research in Britain, circa 1916–1950', *Isis* 101, no. 2 (2010): 285–311; Kieron Flanagan et al., *Lessons from the History of UK Science Policy* (London: British Academy, 2019); Abigail Woods, *A Manufactured Plague: The History of Foot-and-Mouth Disease in Britain* (London: Routledge, 2004).

[6] Wetherell, *Foundations*, 5.

century and extending into the inter-war period, was largely confined to voluntary and commercial organisations, with limited state involvement following the First World War. The second phase, from the mid-1930s until the 1970s, was the high watershed of government-funded 'scientific governance', marked by joint working between the state and commercial bodies. During this phase, 'governing by science' necessitated viewing daily life through a scientific lens and attempting to eradicate the problem of fire through continuous refinement in laboratory testing as well as the systematic grading of flammable materials.

The third phase, that of 'scientific self-governance', began in the 1970s with the de-prioritisation of routine fire testing by government. Organisations like BRE were subject to growing commercial pressures and an opening up of competition for testing from independent (that is, 'for-profit') laboratories. But Thatcher's government and its successors did not simply abandon their commitment to publicly funding scientific research into fire prevention, particularly given the large number of calamitous multiple-fatality fires during the 1980s. Rather, governments restricted their involvement to special investigations, including supporting research into the fire behaviour of cladding systems as part of a wider investigation into the structural integrity of tower blocks following several fires in higher-risk residential buildings (HRRBs) during the 1990s.

By the present century, housing activists and safety campaigners had exposed major defects in the fire protection of HRRBs but were unable to convince central government of the need to reverse its deregulation of controls. Instead, corporate interests exerted ever greater influence over the standards and rules for compliance. At the start of the twenty-first century, where this chapter ends because of the twenty-year closure rule on official archival records, government support for fire research had all but disappeared and the remnants of its scientific civil service had been privatised. BRE had become, describes Stuart Hodkinson, 'a highly commercial organisation embedded in the private building and materials industry' rather than a public body that defined its work as central to the national interest.[7] When it came to fire safety, successive governments were less interested in governing by scientific expertise, but increasingly governed in spite of it.

The emergence of fire testing

The earliest improvements to standards of fire resistance drew together organisations from across the public and private sectors during the late nineteenth and early twentieth centuries. Various attempts were made by

[7] Hodkinson, *Safe*, 41.

private and commercial bodies to generate public interest in fire safety and to increase standards of protection. Notable examples included the Fire Offices Committee (FOC), founded in 1868 to represent the insurance industry, and the British Fire Prevention Committee (BFPC), a subscription association established in 1897. They conducted investigations independently of each other – the BFPC at its London testing station and the FOC at premises in Manchester – and lobbied for greater synchronicity in standards of fire prevention at a time when their work was of growing national significance. This was especially true towards the end of the First World War when the Ministry of Reconstruction, headed by the progressive politician Dr Christopher Addison, advocated directing additional resources towards reducing national fire losses, which he estimated at £10 million annually. As head of what is described as 'a laboratory of new ideas and of social experiment', Addison was particularly anxious about the coalition government's emergency housing programme, commissioning the BFPC to run fire-endurance tests involving concrete slabs, the results of which underpinned housing policy well into the 1920s.[8]

Of greatest significance in the emerging state patronage of scientific governance was the Department of Scientific and Industrial Research (DSIR), formed in 1916. The DSIR provided infrastructural support and funding for programmes of 'public science' recognised as being in the national interest and falling outside the purview of the armed services. Staffed by scientific civil servants, the DSIR's chief focus for the bulk of its existence was to ensure an adequate supply of resources for industry and to coordinate the efficient expenditure of money, time and effort on what Sabine Clarke calls 'fundamental research'; that is, research into issues of society and the economy which affected 'a range of interests wider than a single trade' while also having a 'direct bearing on the health, well-being, or the safety of the whole population'. Fire was inevitably included in this remit, initially as part of the DSIR's Building Research Station (BRS), which was formed in 1921 to lead research into construction and materials.[9]

---

[8] TNA HO/45/15071, Ministry of Reconstruction, 26 April 1918; TNA DSIR/36/4267, Progress Reports, January 1919; Kenneth and Jane Morgan, *Portrait of a Progressive: The Political Career of Christopher, Viscount Addison* (New York: Oxford University Press, 1980), 71.

[9] Andrew Hull, 'War of Words: The Public Science of the British Scientific Community and the Origins of the Department of Scientific and Industrial Research, 1914–16', *British Journal for the History of Science* 32, no. 4 (1999): 461–81; Clarke, 'Pure Science', 301.

A coordinated approach to fire research developed from the mid-1920s with the opening of new testing stations, with capacity for conducting large-scale tests according to agreed standards. The BRS, which started its work at a small premises bequeathed by the Ministry of Health in West London (Addison had since become the first minister of health), soon moved to larger premises at Garston, outside London, to reflect its growing responsibilities. The FOC opened negotiations with the DSIR in 1933 to relocate to Garston so as to benefit from government support and avoid the unnecessary expense of converting its Manchester premises to conform to the British Standard on Fire Resistance (BS 476/1932), published in 1932, which specified rigorous measures that placed British testing on a par with that of leading foreign laboratories. Calls for greater uniformity and rigour were demanded by a number of bodies, including the London County Council and Royal Institute of British Architects.[10]

Later amended, BS 476/1932 was a foundational document in British fire engineering because it established the principles of functionality and classification that dominated the next half-century and more. That it was also cited in expert testimony presented to the Grenfell Inquiry illustrates the longer 'path to Grenfell' through regulatory testing and its subsequent deregulation.[11] Materials would only be accepted as fire resistant if their use permitted the structure as a whole to continue functioning for a specified period while on fire. In practice, this meant that a room had to withstand flames to allow its occupants to exit safely and for the fire brigade to access the building. To enable this, BS 476/1932 appended tests for structures and materials as well as a sliding scale of fire resistance, ranging from Grade A, which provided protection for six hours, to E, which only provided 30 minutes' protection. From 1935, a testing station, jointly funded by the FOC and DSIR, was opened in the up-and-coming town of Borehamwood in outer-north London, emblematic of the growing significance of the southeast to the country's economic prosperity. Testing would henceforth occur in purpose-built temperature-controlled furnaces in order to ascertain the fire behaviour of life-size replica models of buildings, and was based on models developed in North America and Scandinavia, demonstrating the growing internationalisation of fire research as well as the British government's lag.[12]

---

[10] DSIR/FOC negotiations are in TNA DSIR/4.

[11] GTI, LBYP20000001/52, Bisby, 'Phase 2', 53.

[12] *British Standard Definitions for Fire Resistance, Incombustibility, and Noninflammability of Building Materials and Structures, Including Methods of Test, No.476* (London: British Standards Institution, 1932).

The ascendancy of jointly funded fire research

Wartime fire research passed to the Ministry of Home Security after it became apparent that the main threat to Britain's defence came from incendiary bombs dropped from the air.[13] Much was learned from the Blitz about radiant heat and the residual strength of structures damaged by fire, while the DSIR's Chemical Research Laboratory developed foams for fighting deadly oil fires. The Fire Grading Committee's (FGC's) research into structural fire resistance, which started in 1935 but was suspended in 1939, resumed in 1942 to prepare for the mammoth task of post-war reconstruction.[14]

Reflecting its newfound significance to the nation and the urgency of developing cross-government fire policy, the FGC recruited its members from multiple departments. Its 1946 report recommended a radical departure from existing practice in determining the fire risks of different types of building structures and materials. This achieved two broad outcomes: firstly, greater precision in assessing structural risk; secondly, in laying the groundwork for greater standardisation in building across the country (as seen in Chapter 1). In its appendix, the FGC also published a new test for measuring the speed of flame spread across a surface, after recognising the threat posed by the growing use of combustible wall and ceiling linings, which were being deployed in the government's emergency housing programme to bypass shortages in skilled labour and materials.[15]

The new test, an updated version of BS 476/1932, specified that materials were to be placed at right angles to a purpose-built furnace in order to simulate conditions in a corridor or staircase. Following exposure to heat from a gas burner, materials were classified into four groups according to the distance of flame travel: class I included materials with lowest flame spread, while class IV covered those with the greatest spread in the shortest period of time. While class III materials could be used in living rooms and bedrooms under certain conditions, they were never to be permitted for use in staircases or corridors; class IV materials – which included all untreated timbers and building boards – were subject to stricter limits and required treating with flame-retardant paints before use.[16]

---

[13] Ewen, *Fighting Fires*, 131–2.

[14] TNA DSIR/4/77, 'A Description of the Work of the Department of Scientific and Industrial Research', undated, 35.

[15] *Department of Scientific and Industrial Research Report for the Year 1947–48*, Cmd. 7761 (London: HMSO, 1949), 68.

[16] Joint Committee of the Building Research Board, *Fire Grading of Buildings Part I: General Principles and Structural Precautions* (London: HMSO, 1946).

The FGC thus established the principle that the most important part of a building's passive defence was the corridor and staircase, and that compartmentation was crucial in minimising the risk of flame spread; this principle governed the subsequent development of HRRBs across Britain from the mid-1950s, which were commonly fitted with a single staircase. To supplement this, fire alarms, extinguishers and dry risers would be fitted in public areas. This eventually evolved into the 'stay put' policy, published as a British Standard Code of Practice in 1962 and revised in 1971 following the collapse of Ronan Point. The code of practice informed residents that 'You will normally be safe to stay within your flat' so long as windows and doors were closed. Residents should only leave the premises 'in the unlikely event of smoke or heat entering the flat'. 'Stay put', then, was predicated on the view that evacuation was no longer necessary because of 'the high degree of compartmentation provided in dwellings in modern blocks'. Yet, while this once meant that 'the spread of fire and smoke from one dwelling to another and the need to evacuate the occupants of adjoining dwellings are unusual', the policy's catastrophic failure in 2017 proved that public faith in its ability to protect residents of tower blocks had been fatally undermined.[17]

Securing a balance between safety and cost was left to the Joint Fire Research Organisation (JFRO), funded by the DSIR and FOC. As 'a novel experiment in administration', JFRO had two goals: to devise a national programme of research into fire defence and to collect and publish statistics of fires attended by fire brigades on behalf of the Home Office. JFRO was designed from the outset to pool the available expertise in managing public science, with a board composed of architects, physicists, chemists and firefighters. Day-to-day management of its Fire Research Station (FRS) was devolved to a director of research, who was required to combine technical expertise with administrative acumen. Successive directors, all male, were considered to be safe pairs of hands with experience in line managing staff within the scientific civil service; as members of the scientific class, they were highly qualified graduates, with 'the right sort of active, enquiring and constructive mind' and the ability to direct innovative projects.[18]

The station's inaugural director was S.H. Clarke, who arrived from the Ministry of Home Security along with Viscount Falmouth, the first chairman of the board. Clarke developed the FRS's testing facilities before leaving a

---

[17] *British Standard Code of Practice CP 3: Chapter IV – Precautions against Fire. Part 1: Flats and Maisonettes* (London: BSI, 1971), 5, 34.

[18] Department of Scientific and Industrial Research, *Report for the Year 1947–8*, Cmd. 7761 (London: HMSO, 1949), 36–7; Harry Melville, *The Department of Scientific and Industrial Research* (London: George Allen & Unwin, 1962), 60, 158–61.

decade later to manage the DSIR's fuel laboratory. His successor, Dennis Lawson, lectured in physics at Woolwich Polytechnic before his appointment in 1948 as a principal scientific officer. As director, Lawson oversaw the continued expansion and diversification of the FRS's research, particularly into consumer protection, and co-authored forty technical papers published between 1953 and 1972. During its first twenty-five years, the FRS's most senior research staff shaped the nascent discipline of fire engineering and solidified the elastic links between the public and private sectors. Two examples stand out: first, Dr David Rasbash, who, having first joined the station in 1948, was appointed professor of fire engineering at the University of Edinburgh in 1973 in a move recently described as 'the first time that technical knowledge, need, and experiential learning converged'.[19] Second, Margaret Law, a graduate in physics and mathematics from the University of London, joined the FRS in 1952 and became a specialist in fire dynamics before moving into consultancy work for Ove Arup Partnership in the 1970s. A recipient of several professional accolades, including a stint as visiting professor in fire safety engineering at the University of Greenwich, Law was instrumental in bringing fire science into the everyday practice of the design engineer and inspiring other female fire engineers like Dr Barbara Lane, who gave expert testimony to the Grenfell Tower Inquiry, to enter what was predominantly (and indeed still remains) a male-dominated field. That Law features on the cover of the FRS's 1952 annual report indicates the novelty of appointing a female scientist a few years after the civil service had removed the marriage bar.[20]

The contested nature of fire research

The FRS's annual reports reveal both its growing workload during the 1950s and 1960s and its tangible contribution to society. Its scientists contributed materially to improved public health and graded the combustibility of building materials. They also investigated the conditions in which a growing variety of domestic consumer goods (including heaters, kitchen appliances and television sets) were operated, occasionally with disastrous effects,

[19] Dougal Drysdale and Jack Watts, 'David Rasbash and the Department of Fire Engineering', *Fire Safety Science News* 35 (2013): 14–15; GTI, JTOR00000006/82, José L. Torero, 'Phase 2 Grenfell Tower Inquiry: Adequacy of the Current Testing Regime', 4 January 2022, 83.

[20] Peter Johnson and Barbara Lane, 'In Memoriam: Professor Margaret Law', *Fire Technology* 53 (2017): 2041–3; *Report of the Fire Research Board for the Year 1952* (London: HMSO, 1953); Helen Glew, *Gender, Rhetoric and Regulation: Women's Work in the Civil Service and the London County Council, 1900–55* (Manchester: Manchester University Press, 2016).

thereby acting as a precursor to the emergence of consumer protection. Its physicists also modelled the likely fire damage caused to British cities by an atomic bomb, which influenced emergency preparedness planning into the late 1960s.[21]

In 1964 the FRS was transferred to the new Ministry of Technology following the election of a Labour Government committed to harnessing 'the white heat' of a 'scientific revolution'. While Prime Minister Harold Wilson was sensitive to complaints that his government restricted innovation through new building controls, he famously warned in an earlier speech of the danger of 'an unregulated private enterprise economy', which would lead Britain to become 'a stagnant backwater, pitied and condemned by the rest of the world'. A highly educated workforce was a flagship element of his government's industrial policy, while an expanded scientific civil service was 'part of our national planning' in balancing innovation and wealth creation with greater equality of opportunity and improved health and safety.[22] Fire research was a small but significant feature of Wilson's vision for greater precision and skill in building a stronger economy. Investment in university-trained physicists, chemists and statisticians was important if record fire losses, which exceeded £66 million in 1963 (approximately £1.4 billion in 2022) and were predicted to rise in 1964, were to be brought under greater control. Estimated losses for January 1964 alone were nearly £7.75 million, one of the highest monthly totals since records began. As one insurance official described it, fire damage was 'a grossly expensive bonfire and one the nation cannot afford for long'.[23]

Although scientists would tackle the fire problem by subjecting it to greater precision and measurement, scientific governance remained a contested arena throughout the post-war period, especially where it was seen to challenge commercial interests. Criticism was most trenchant from manufacturers, commonly centring on the costs of compliance. The FRS, they complained, took a narrow view on fire safety, defining it through a purely scientific lens at the expense of its economic costs, which stifled product innovation. This was a particular complaint, as we saw in Chapter 1, in the building industry where 'deemed to satisfy' regulations specified restrictions on the use of flammable materials in certain parts of buildings.

---

[21] A comprehensive run of Fire Research Notes has been digitised by the International Association for Fire Safety Science and made publicly accessible at the Fire Safety Science Digital Archive, <https://publications.iafss.org/publications/frn/info>, accessed 7 March 2023.

[22] Harold Wilson, 'Labour's Plan for Science', 1 October 1963.

[23] *Financial Times*, 28 February 1964, 12.

But given fire research was managed by a joint board of public and private sector actors working in the national interest, it is difficult to sympathise with industry complaints.

There were stinging criticisms from construction product manufacturers of the surface-spread-of-flame test. While it remained the most reliable testing method into the 1960s, it produced an incomplete measure of the effect of a single material on the growth of fire. Problems were first encountered in the 1940s with the poor fire performance of internal lining materials, specifically wooden fibre building boards. These materials had emerged as a cheap mass-produced alternative to plaster and, with low thermal conductivity and high sound absorption, were widely used for lining post-war council houses, schools and factories. Marian Bowley recorded an 'extraordinarily rapid' growth of fibreboard in building in the decade after 1945, with rates of growth ranging between 48 and 175 per cent. However, alarm bells sounded as early as 1947 following several fires in council-built bungalows lined with combustible building boards, which caused problems for tenants to escape. One such fire, involving the death of an infant, culminated with the coroner complaining that he had 'never been in any building in my life which has had the appearance of being more ready to be burned than this'.[24]

The FRS responded by conducting surface-flame tests and, in 1949, large-scale fire-endurance experiments involving houses of post-war design, one of which was lined with exposed fibreboard while the other contained fibreboard plastered over. The results revealed wide disparities in the flashover times: in the house with exposed linings a safe exit was impossible within 6.5 minutes of the fire starting, while this extended to more than 26 minutes in the plasterboard-lined house. Regulations stipulated that internal partitions separating rooms from the stairs, landings and floors should give 30 minutes' protection against fire. Low-density fibre building boards were subsequently rated as class IV, one of the worst-performing materials, and excluded from the list of materials suitable for use in council housing.[25]

The building-board industry, which had hitherto shown little interest in improving the safety of its products, unsurprisingly mobilised in defence of what had become a multi-million-pound industry since the end of the war. The Fibre Building Board Development Organisation (FIDOR) counteracted the FRS's data through publicity and lobbying. Sympathetic

[24] Marian Bowley, *Innovations in Building Materials: An Economic Study* (London: Gerald Duckworth, 1960), 346; *Daily Mail*, 25 January 1947, 3; 14 February 1947, 1; 13 March 1948, 3.
[25] *Report of the Fire Research Board for the Year 1950* (London: HMSO, 1951), 1–2, 24–8.

articles appeared in newspapers emphasising the industry's contribution to economic recovery and stressing that the industry was not complacent in improving its products, while MPs were paid to lobby within Westminster.[26] FIDOR also criticised the government's supposed overreaction on the basis that unprotected fibreboard was rarely used in houses, but was normally plastered over to cover the joints and reduce the fire risk to the same level as 'many other materials which have hitherto been considered to be "safer"'.[27] This does not appear to have been universally the case, however, as serious fires in Bristol's council houses in the 1960s, involving untreated wooden-board partitions, caused 'extremely severe and abnormal' levels of damage and led to council workers plastering over boards in 680 council houses at a cost exceeding £82,000. With the introduction of Building Regulations, for Scotland in 1963 and England and Wales two years later, restrictions on the use of combustible internal linings were further tightened, which again shows the benefit of regulations when properly enforced.[28]

While their motives may have differed, industry bodies and scientists agreed that greater precision was required to accurately measure the contribution made by materials to a fire's growth. Trials, part-funded by FIDOR, led to the creation of a flame propagation test in 1968. This test involved exposing a specimen sample to gas burners and radiant electric bars contained in a combustion chamber for up to 20 minutes; performance was expressed as a numerical index with values indicating the rate of heat release. The propagation test had two consequences: first, it was easily replicated by commercial testing stations rather than having to rely on the larger furnaces of the FRS. This consequently reduced the costs of testing while redistributing them from the taxpayer to the market; second, by ascertaining the rate of heat transfer, the test enabled the finer grading of materials as class 0, thereby permitting their use when treated with fire-retardant chemicals. BS 476-6:1968 proved to be especially useful when measuring flame spread between different storeys within a building, which meant it was later adopted in routine tests involving multi-storey buildings, the majority performed by private testing laboratories in Cheshire (by Warrington Research Centre) and Buckinghamshire (by the Timber Research Development Association, later renamed Chiltern International Fire) from the 1970s. The precedent had been established that the private sector should play a greater role in product testing and approval as well as in the monitoring of regulatory standards; fire research

---

[26] *Financial Times*, 4 February 1954, 8.
[27] *The Builder*, 4 September 1964, 497–8.
[28] *The Times*, 31 December 1963, 6; *Financial Times*, 23 November 1965, 15.

was entering a new era of scientific self-governance and it was unsurprising to see senior scientific civil servants being headhunted by industry, at a higher salary than they could command in the public sector, during the 1970s and 1980s.[29]

Consumer safety

While the FRS's early work focused on building materials, it diversified into consumer safety from the mid-1950s. The widespread availability of labour-saving devices such as cookers and electric irons has been recognised by historians as a cornerstone of the new consumerist society, first in 1930s middle-class homes, then in working-class households from the 1950s. The revolution in electrical appliances brought science into domestic life and transformed the mid-twentieth-century home into a controlled space engineered for safety as much as comfort and convenience. Post-war council houses and flats were designed with functionality and modernity in mind, with kitchens positioned as 'central to healthier, more hygienic and less labour-intensive forms of living'.[30] Firms and the state increasingly drew upon the skills of the scientist and the engineer to design safety into new products, which was the consequence of heightened 'consumer consciousness' and a demand for a participatory style of consumer politics.[31]

New consumer goods were not without their risks, of course, as the Ronan Point explosion proved so catastrophically. In this case, the tenant of the flat in which the explosion occurred, Ivy Hodge, was called to give evidence to the all-male inquiry, despite clearly being traumatised by her experience and suffering from burns injuries. Pictured by one newspaper heavily bandaged and flanked by a nurse, Hodge was questioned about her decision to ask a neighbour to install her electric cooker rather than a qualified electrician. Her burnt-out cooker was subject to intensive laboratory tests by FRS officials before it was brought into the courtroom as evidence of the devastating consequences of an ill-fitted appliance.[32] 'Scientific governance' had thus brought the home into the public domain of the courtroom, opening up that previously private space to expert scrutiny

---

[29] B.F.W. Rogowski, 'The Fire Propagation Test: Its Development and Application', *FR Note* (London: HMSO, 1970).

[30] Catriona Beaumont, *Housewives and Citizens: Domesticity and the Women's Movement in England, 1928–64* (Manchester: Manchester University Press, 2013), 189–214; Sean Nixon, 'Life in the Kitchen: Television Advertising, the Housewife and Domestic Modernity in Britain, 1955–1969', *Contemporary British History* 31, no. 1 (2017): 70.

[31] Matthew Hilton, 'The Death of a Consumer Society', *Transactions of the Royal Historical Society* 18 (2008): 218.

[32] *Daily Express*, 19 June 1968, 7.

and media speculation in a practice that has been replicated countless times since, including during Phase 1 of the Grenfell Inquiry where the Hotpoint fridge-freezer in the kitchen of Flat 16 in which the fire originated was subject to forensic attention before its owner was absolved of any blame. In both cases, the offending appliance was pictured in newspapers and official reports and the insinuation that they had been poorly fitted or tampered with lingered after both parties had been absolved of blame.[33]

The wider social benefits of fire science were perhaps best exemplified by space heaters, which attracted considerable public attention during the post-war years following several fatal fires involving children. Scientific interest was piqued by statistical evidence which showed that the number of fires involving paraffin heaters was increasing at a greater rate than the domestic consumption of paraffin. In 1950, there were 300 fires nationally in which oil heaters were the probable cause; by 1957, this figure had risen to 1,300. Of these, 1,075 involved portable appliances. The following year, 1958, saw the figures rise to a startling 4,464 fires, of which 23 per cent were accounted for by portable drip-feed oil heaters flaring or overheating.[34] Firefighters and trade unions repeatedly raised the ubiquity of cheap mass-produced heaters in homes as a concern. Aimed at working-class households, drip-feed heaters inexpensively warmed homes during the winter, but at a risk, not least from the fact that households would keep a supply of paraffin tucked away at home. Invoking wartime rhetoric, the Fire Brigades Union quoted calls for safeguards to prevent draughts from 'turning apparently innocent oil stoves into incendiary bombs'.[35]

Government only acted following a gruesome fire in a council house in Ware, another growing town in outer London, which claimed the lives of five children aged between two and nine years. Dennis Lawson, newly appointed director of the FRS, was summoned to attend the inquest where he reported that tests on drip-feed heaters revealed how quickly flames spread with a small draught. In this case, the father of the children had briefly left the front door ajar while buying provisions from the grocery van, which caused the heater to topple and the flames to spread instantaneously, cutting his children off from rescue.[36]

---

[33] *Newham Recorder*, 7 November 1968, 1; Hugh Griffiths, *Report of the Inquiry into the Collapse of Flats at Ronan Point, Canning Town* (London: HMSO, 1968), 7–8; Moore-Bick, *Phase 1 Report*, 505–15.

[34] Hansard (Commons), 15 March 1960, 1124.

[35] *The Firefighter*, December 1959, 22; TNA HLG/117/200, Correspondence between Terence Parry, FBU general secretary, and Ministry of Housing and Local Government, concerning the provision of fire-guard wall fittings in new-build homes.

[36] *The Times*, 14 November 1959, 6.

Having heard the evidence, the jury returned a verdict of accidental death, adding a rider urging manufacturers to take all measures to remove dangers and issue public warnings. The coroner recommended government to urgently consider legislating before further deaths occurred. Indicating the public interest in the fire, daily newspapers reported at length from the inquest, albeit using different tropes in their coverage. While a broadsheet paper like *The Times* reported verbatim the proceedings of the inquest, the *Daily Express*, until recently Britain's most popular newspaper, published a pictorial report on the tests to stress the urgency of the peril facing homes equipped with oil heaters. The accompanying article emphasised the risk posed to its readers ('Why this matters to YOU'), deploying typically gendered language: 'in 90 seconds, a reasonable time for a housewife to have her front door open while she pays the milkman, the heater blew up'. As historians have shown, popular daily newspapers increasingly championed domestic consumption from the 1950s, particularly targeting female readers. Managing a safe but comfortable home remained the responsibility of the dutiful housewife, even if, in this case, the father had caused the accident.[37]

In the months that followed the inquest, Lawson oversaw further tests. His report concluded that drip-feed radiant oil heaters presented 'a severe fire hazard' if exposed to a draught of 3.3 miles per hour or above. The director of the British Safety Council, Leonard Hodge, followed this up with a call for the 'tens of thousands' of defective heaters to be recalled, stating 'the sooner the public gets something safe and not just an incendiary bomb the better'.[38] Support emanated from the government's backbenches, with Conservative MP Gerald Nabarro noting that 'A speed of 3.3 m.p.h. is slower than the speed at which I walk through the Lobby.' Not only was Nabarro able to set an impressive pace on foot but he also promoted a Private Member's Bill, under Parliament's Ten Minute Rule, introducing minimum standards of safety in domestic oil-burning appliances. MPs from across the House united over their shock at the events in the Ware case and a copycat blaze which caused fatal burns to two children in Nottingham in early 1960. The outcome, the Oil Burners (Standards) Act 1960, was a rare instance of a Private Bill passing into law with cross-party support and proved that positive change could be effected when politicians

---

[37] *The Times*, 3 December 1959, 8; *Daily Express*, 9 March 1960, 5; Adrian Bingham and Martin Conboy, *Tabloid Century: The Popular Press in Britain, 1896 to the Present* (Oxford: Peter Lang, 2015), 184–5.

[38] Joint Fire Research Organisation, *Effects of Draughts on the Burning of Portable Oil Heaters* (London: HMSO, 1960); *The Times*, 8 March 1960, 7; 9 March 1960, 5.

were prepared to act boldly. Firefighters welcomed the action, even if it was years overdue.[39]

New safety regulations were quickly issued by the home secretary, and adopted by the Oil Appliance Manufacturers Association, which caused a slowing in the rate of fires and injuries caused by upturned heaters.[40] Some local authorities, listening to manufacturers' concerns, issued guidelines warning against tenant misuse of heaters in council houses. The Royal Borough of Kensington and Chelsea issued rules governing the use of storage heaters for residents of its new Lancaster West Estate in the mid-1970s. Its local tenants' association warned residents not to tamper with the heaters without expert advice, noting that some people received hospital treatment for scalds from doing so.[41] This combination of expert and lay voices coalesced to pressure central government into action to protect those least able to protect themselves. The era of scientific governance accepted the merits of government intervention when it was underpinned by up-to-date scientific research that stood up to public scrutiny. The FRS had materially contributed to public safety, which makes the later dilution of its responsibilities all the more disappointing.

The era of scientific self-governance

The ascendancy of the FRS was short-lived because it was an easy target for funding cuts and privatisation during the 1970s and 1980s. With starting capital costs of £100,000 and running costs of only £50,000 in the late 1940s, by the mid-1950s its budget had been modestly increased to £125,000. Fire research contributed a small proportion of the DSIR's overall expenditure on research, with five to six times more spent on building and roads. Given its unique funding arrangement, JFRO was relaxed in allowing manufacturing associations to provide financial support for testing. By 1970, following a significant expansion in its remit over the previous decade, the FRS, now spending approximately £540,000 each year, had a steadily increasing income of £74,000 from consultancy work.[42]

By the 1970s, however, the FOC's contribution had fallen to one-third of the station's annual running costs. This growing disparity led to

---

[39] *The Times*, 8 March 1960, 12; Hansard (Commons), 15 March 1960, 1124; *The Firefighter*, May 1960, 5.

[40] *Financial Times*, 17 September 1960, 6.

[41] RBKCA Acc/2001/003/Box 24, 'Newssheet of the Lancaster West Tenants' Association', November 1976, 5.

[42] Figures are taken from the DSIR's annual reports, available via UK Parliamentary Papers.

proposals to reduce government support for routine testing. In 1972 the FRS was merged with the BRS and the Forest Products Research Laboratory to create BRE, and placed under the control of the new bureaucratic monolith, the Department of the Environment (DoE), which started negotiations to transfer routine testing to the private sector.[43] There was some logic to merging building and fire research and the FRS's scientists continued to contribute to the mitigation of fire losses over the next decade. While only approximately 40 per cent of the total number of fires occurred in buildings, they were responsible for over 85 per cent of casualties and more than 95 per cent of damage. According to figures published by the British Insurance Association, national fire losses amounted to £120.4 million in 1969 and £176 million four years later (more than £2 billion today). With greater emphasis placed on the economics of fire safety, the FRS developed a cost–benefit model that underpinned successive governments' resourcing of the fire service. The costs of fire protection were assessed alongside the value of property and life at risk in order to determine the best allocation of public resources to early detection as well as prevention and protection. This included determining the cost of enforcing fire precautions legislation, estimated at £37 million per annum in the mid-1970s, which was used to justify the introduction of competition in building control and reduction in fire service enforcement powers during the 1980s.[44]

Following the introduction of the customer/contractor principle across government, the FRS was also required to subject its work to greater financial scrutiny, recruiting customers from industry as well as government. Many of its projects were commissioned in the wake of multiple-fatality fires. Its first project as a contractor, commissioned by the Department of Health and Social Security, followed the Coldharbour Hospital fire in 1972 and involved site visits to determine its cause. In the wake of the tragedy, a new type of hospital furniture and cubicle partitioning incorporating modern safety measures was tested in front of officials.[45]

The Coldharbour fire established a precedent for site investigations following multiple-fatality fires, with the results submitted as evidence to public inquiries. Lessons were learned and the results filtered into decision making in a political system that continued to value scientific governance for non-routine work. But still the FRS had to increase its revenue from such work, especially where it involved research on behalf of customers, as was

[43] *BRE Annual Report* (London: HMSO, 1972), 43.

[44] *BRE Report* (London: HMSO, 1975), 53–5; *Fire Prevention*, April 1970, 5; January 1974, 5.

[45] *BRE Annual Report* (London: HMSO, 1973), v, 36.

the case following the Summerland fire in 1973, and a fire at Woolworths in Manchester in 1979, which killed eleven people because toxic smoke was released by burning furniture filled with polyurethane foam. In 1981, following a fire at the Stardust nightclub in Dublin, in which forty-eight people died, Ireland's government sponsored several laboratories, the FRS included, to assist its Tribunal of Inquiry in ascertaining the cause and spread of the blaze. The FRS ran a series of *ad hoc* tests to reproduce the early stages of the fire, combining experiments on simulations of parts of the original building, before culminating with a full-scale experiment on a model replica of the club.[46]

If the FRS played a key role in understanding multiple-fatality fires, the impetus towards a greater level of scientific self-governance continued with the routine testing of materials, goods and fire protection equipment. Some of the changes pre-dated the 1979 general election, which resonates with James Vernon's findings about the outsourcing of services at Heathrow Airport from the late 1960s; clearly it is insufficient to equate deregulation and privatisation exclusively with the Thatcher governments of 1979–90.[47] Privatisation accelerated in 1976 following the dissolution of JFRO, with the transfer of all routine testing and a number of FRS staff to the FOC's Fire Insurers' Research and Testing Organisation. Laboratories such as Warrington Research Centre undertook responsibility for routine tests, with the results hidden from public view because of commercial confidentiality.[48] Fire science was therefore one of the first parts of the post-war social infrastructure to be dismantled, creating a culture of secrecy and mistrust between the privatised fire sector and public fire service, which intensified in the decades that followed. As the Grenfell Tower Inquiry learned, tests conducted in 2001 by privately run laboratories revealed the combustibility of polyethylene-core aluminium composite material cladding, but the results, 'bound by confidentiality', were withheld from public dissemination until it was too late.[49]

This era of scientific self-governance took place against a backdrop of squeezed public sector finances and the marketisation of public services. As industry was encouraged to manage its own affairs, it is unsurprising to see

---

[46] *Report of the Tribunal of Inquiry on the Fire at the Stardust, Artane, Dublin on the 14th February, 1981* (Dublin: Stationery Office, 1982). The FRS's investigations are documented in TNA DSIR/4/3859.

[47] Vernon, 'Heathrow', 213–47.

[48] *Fire Prevention*, November 1976, 6.

[49] See, eg, GTI, Testimony of Dr Deborah Smith, BRE, 21 February 2022, 156.

the fire protection industry assume greater responsibility for determining risk across the sector. BRE was now required to demonstrate value for money by reducing staff costs: whereas in 1976 BRE employed 1,349 staff, with 227 based at the FRS, by the end of 1980 staffing had been cut to 975 and 159, respectively. Redundancies were accompanied by a consequent narrowing in the scope of research, with the FRS concentrating on pure research and site investigations; the Home Office took responsibility for the production of fire statistics from 1976, with the statisticians transferring to its staff in 1984. By the end of the decade, BRE's staff numbers had fallen to 654, with 101 working at the FRS.[50]

Alongside staffing changes, initiatives were introduced to make BRE more 'business-like' by adopting private sector management techniques. By the end of 1982–3, the FRS earned over £120,000 in income from industry for sponsored research and advisory services. A Technical Consultancy was created in 1988 to attract industry funding. Its new director, Roger Courtney, boasted of BRE's growing commercial potential in 'preparing for a future in which its clients, in both Government and industry, will be using BRE not only for its technical excellence, but because it offers the best value for money' to overseas markets.[51]

One of the Technical Consultancy's first commissions was to assess the smoke control design proposed for redeveloping Battersea Power Station into a leisure park. An innovative computer modelling programme called JASMINE ('[J] Analysis of Smoke Movement In Enclosures') predicted the effects of fire on buildings without having to resort to burning full-scale replicas. The development of electronic computers stimulated a refinement in the modelling of fire, drawing together researchers from across the public and private sectors to predict fire behaviour in prescribed situations. This had far-reaching implications for building control, as the FRS recognised following controversial reforms to the Building Regulations in 1985.[52] The financial and time savings promised by computer modelling attracted policymakers. From 2007, 'full-scale test data' was permitted to predict fire performance, which was interpreted as allowing for the use of desktop studies because of their use of 'test data' instead of full-scale

[50] Hansard (Commons), 21 March 1980, 366; 17 June 1981, 384; 8 December 1982, 564; 14 January 1987, 183.

[51] Hansard (Commons), 27 April 1983, 333; BRE, *Annual Report* (London: HMSO, 1988), 3; BRE, *Annual Review* (Garston: BRE, 1991), 3.

[52] BRE, *Annual Review* (London: HMSO, 1989), 19.

tests in burn halls or laboratories.[53] As a result of changes to the published guidance, manufacturing firms could commission a succession of desktop studies in order to secure approval for their construction products. This was permissible even in cases where a manufacturer's product had failed *in situ* physical tests, as was revealed during the Grenfell Inquiry where one firm commissioned a total of twenty-nine desktop studies to secure approval for its insulation product using data obtained from an earlier failed test.[54] For many in central government and the construction industry, flexibility was the preferred way of ensuring regulatory compliance, which reveals a gradual but perceptible shift from the laboratory to the computer suite in determining fire behaviour and assessing acceptable risks to human life.

The development of computer modelling did not fully replace full-scale fire tests overnight, however. Indeed, it cohabited alongside conventional methods, including physical testing and field investigation, particularly with the emerging problem of multi-storey building fires. Public concerns about the safety of HRRBs were first raised following the Ronan Point explosion in 1968 when metropolitan local authorities across the country made use of site visits and surveys to assess the safety of their own tower blocks.[55] The FRS investigated the incidence of fires in post-war multi-storey flats in London, finding 'no evidence that occupants of the flats are more likely to be trapped than those in other dwellings', which justified the continued use of the 'stay put' policy by fire brigades.[56] Fears dramatically escalated in the 1970s following several overseas fires involving large loss of life. Even then, the overwhelming consensus was that the residents of Britain's tower blocks were safer owing to a combination of good design and regulatory compliance. Yet problems persisted, not least in the discrepancy between the growing vogue for high-rise living and the contradictory messages around evacuation. In one case, a fire at a block of flats in Brent, northwest London, in 1975 led to the death of a thirty-year-old male after London Fire Brigade's ladders were found to be too short to rescue him from his thirteenth-floor balcony flat. This fire led to the revision of official advice on 'stay put' by a working group for the Central Fire Brigades Advisory

---

[53] FBU, *Grenfell Tower Fire*, 18; Department for Communities and Local Government, *Building Regulations 2000. Fire Safety. Approved Document B* (London: NBS, 2006), 93.

[54] GTI, KINoo022610.09.18, Testimony of Adrian Pargeter, Kingspan Insulation Limited, 4 December 2020, 60.

[55] LMA GLC/AR/ENG/SE/1/8 (1/2) and (2/2), Ronan Point Inquiry.

[56] J.F. Fry, 'Fires in Post-War Multi-Storey Flats in London, 1966', *FR Note* (London: HMSO, 1971), 73.

Council (CFBAC), warning against using balconies 'unless they form part of an escape route'.[57]

Clearly lessons were still being learned and acted upon to avoid ambiguous messaging and help save lives as part of the micro-politics of the state's regulation of its citizens during emergencies. Fire safety policymaking was, in this sense, experiential and embodied practice in that it responded to cases where the limitations of 'stay put' were exposed by building design or the state's limited protective resources. 'Stay put' inevitably came in for criticism – from housing activists, firefighters and residents alike – in cases where frontline firefighters were unable to safely reach occupants trapped in multi-storey buildings. Meanwhile, national advisory bodies like the CFBAC – which enjoyed a wide representation of interested bodies speaking on behalf of frontline firefighters as well as employers and senior officers – played important roles in reflexively learning from incidents such as these, thereby contributing to longer-term improvements in public safety.

The high-rise fire risk became more prominent during the 1980s with the vogue for over-cladding and the structural issues that beset individual tower blocks were upscaled to a national crisis by the turn of the present century. Problems posed by damp and rain penetration in local authority Large Panel System housing created the need for improved thermal insulation by over-cladding masonry walls with a variety of materials ranging from rock or glass fibre to combustible thermoplastics. One such building, the twenty-four-storey block of council-owned flats at Royston Hill in Glasgow, built in the late 1960s, suffered a fire, fortunately without casualties, in 1988. Post-fire investigations revealed not only that the refurbishment had compromised the building's structural resistance but also, in a move that resonates with the experiences of Grenfell Tower's residents, that tenants had been repeatedly ignored when they raised legitimate concerns with the council's housing department. Two years before the fire, warnings had been issued in Adam Curtis's documentary for the BBC, *The Great British Housing Disaster*, that the flats failed to meet structural regulations to withstand a main gas explosion and thus posed a 'very obvious' fire risk, while laboratory tests revealed 'a risk of increased vertical fire spread' in over-cladding systems; the flats were subsequently demolished.[58]

[57] Read, 'Fire Risks', 3; *The Times*, 5 February 1975, 2; *British Standard Code of Practice CP3*, 34.
[58] GTI, SWE00000001/70, Witness Statement, Sam Webb, 4 March 2022, 71; F.W. Rogowski, R. Ramaprasad and J.R. Southern, *Fire Performance of External Thermal Insulation for Walls of Multi-Storey Buildings* (Garston: BRE, 1988); *New Civil Engineer*, 11 April 1991, in TNA AT/66/389, 'Knowsley Fire'. On the failures of housing providers to

Two later destructive fires further exposed the risks to public safety from tower blocks, bringing existing *ad hoc* local campaign groups together in a national effort to challenge the state's abandonment of its duty of care to high-rise residents. In 1990, a fire at the fifteen-storey Merry Hill Court in Smethwick claimed the life of a resident and highlighted a litany of defects in the tower block's protection, including an absence of fire stops beyond the ninth floor, no fire-proofing of internal gas pipes or ducting and defective dry risers which hampered firefighting efforts. Brian Fuller, the experienced chief of the West Midlands Fire Brigade, called for greater powers to allow firefighters to issue safety certificates for multi-storey residential schemes following site inspections, but these went unheeded.[59]

Little had seemingly been learned by housing providers from the case at Ronan Point, and it took a rigorous grassroots campaign to force lasting change. The Newham Tower Block Tenants Campaign, armed with a converted double-decker bus that toured local estates to discuss pressing issues with residents, put the issue of Ronan Point back on the agenda. This was supported by data gathered from fire safety tests conducted by Sam Webb and his students which revealed the tower block to be structurally unsound. Eventually, following extensive media coverage at the national and local levels, the local authority agreed to dismantle the tower block and rehouse all residents as well as commit to improving conditions for all tower-block residents in Newham. 'Good riddance Ronan Point!', reported the *Newham News*, alongside a photograph of elated children standing outside the condemned tower under an unfurled banner which read 'VICTORY FOR TENANTS!'[60]

Following a major conference in 1983, with the tagline 'Tower Blocks: Homes Not Prisons', the National Tower Blocks Network (NTBN) was formed as a loose federation of groups and individuals with a shared concern about the quality of life in Britain's tower-block homes. Through information sharing, publicity and encouraging practical solutions to social and structural problems, the NTBN would bring together local campaigners facing similar problems, thereby 'making tower blocks the national issue they deserve to be'.[61] In the aftermath of the Merry Hill Court fire and following a spot survey of five local authority-managed tower blocks across the country, the

---

listen to residents, see Daniel Renwick, 'Organising on Mute', in Bulley, Edkins and El-Enany, *After Grenfell*, 19–22.

[59] *Building*, 20 July 1990, 11, in TNA AT/66/389.

[60] *Newham News*, June 1986, 1, in NBA VF/NEW/728; ESCH 2019_esch_RoPo_03, Interview with Frances Clarke, 8 March 2019; ESCH 2018_esch_RoPo_04, Interview with Webb.

[61] National Tower Block Conference, 23 October 1983, <https://www.towerblocksuk .com>, accessed 7 March 2023.

NTBN issued a call for urgent government-funded research into the fire per-formance of over-cladding systems and encouraged residents to organise in support of a national fire safety charter for flats. Residents and housing activists would no longer trust government and other official bodies to dictate the pace of change within the sector in a move that was mirrored by similar developments in the houses in multiple occupancy sector, as the next chapter will show.[62]

The following year, in 1991, a fire in a bin storage area on the ground-floor level spread rapidly up a newly installed rainscreen (a form of sheet-boarding to provide weather protection and improve a building's energy efficiency) over-cladding on the eleven-storey Knowsley Heights in Liverpool. This was, reported the NTBN's newsletter, a £1 million refurbishment project projected as a 'showpiece' for the revitalisation of tower blocks up and down the country, part-funded by central government, but it proved to be nothing more than a showcase for the dangers associated with over-cladding.[63] Fortunately the fire did not extend into the interior of the building and all residents scrambled to safety amidst what was described as 'a towering inferno'.[64] An investigation by the FRS's Fires of Special Interest Section revealed that, while the refurbishment materials met Building Regulations approval, no fire-stopping barriers had been installed in the gap between the cladding and the walls, allowing the fire to spread unchecked upwards in a 'chimney effect' that a firefighter described as 'the most frightening thing any of us has ever seen'.[65] Rather than publicly admit any failings, the government's Housing Management Estates Division, which administered the national cladding programme, requested its press office 'to play down the issue of the fire'. The experience at Knowsley Heights was consequently treated by civil servants as 'insignificant' rather than a forewarning of the risks of over-cladding using proven combustible materials.[66]

Subsequent recommendations by civil servants for 'a major increase' in the use of barriers on similar block refurbishment programmes were fiercely resisted by the over-cladding industry on the grounds of cost.

[62] National Tower Blocks Network, 'Annual Spot Safety Survey' (1990); 'Fire Safety Information Pack' (not dated), <https://www.towerblocksuk.com>, accessed 7 March 2023.
[63] *The View*, spring 1991, 1.
[64] *Liverpool Echo*, 5 April 1991, in TNA AT/66/389.
[65] *Private Eye*, 21 June 1991, 14, in TNA AT/66/389; Grenfell Tower Inquiry, BRE00035385/2, Penny Morgan, Derek Jones and Sharon Clinch, *Summary of Fires Investigated: April 1991 to March 1992* (London: HMSO, 1992). The site investigator, Penny Morgan, appeared before the Grenfell Tower Inquiry: BRE00043866/2, 20 October 2021.
[66] TNA AT/66/389, note by 'Lyn', 16 April 1991; Alison Curtis, 'Knowsley Heights: External Fire on April the 5th 1991', 8 April 1991.

Moreover, industry proposals for a commercial desktop study testing programme were initially rejected by the government in preference for an independent FRS testing rig at Cardington, Bedfordshire. This new four-storey facility would be capable of conducting large-scale tests of over-cladding materials, which would more accurately reveal a fire's performance over a multi-storey block – as well as its impact on the ventilation properties of cladding – than a small-scale test at its existing premises or a desktop study.[67]

This research into over-cladding revealed how much of the FRS's work was not best left to the private sector. As BRE Chief Executive Roger Courtney stated in a 1995 interview, 'The maintenance of the knowledge base is fundamentally a non-commercial operation ... We can't have people thinking we are pursuing some commercial agenda of our own.'[68] Yet BRE's future as a public body faced ever greater scrutiny from John Major's Conservative Government in its programme to extend deregulation in the name of improving national competitiveness. In 1994 legislation paved the way for the further removal of 'barriers to trade', while an Efficiency Unit was tasked with recommending proposals for removing government controls; its research establishments were one such area earmarked for privatisation.[69]

Eventually, in February 1997 government sold BRE to a management bid team, rejecting a similar bid from University College London which would have retained its public service ethos. A registered charity, the Foundation for the Built Environment (later renamed the BRE Trust), took ownership, with the board, chaired by Courtney, recruiting its members from the fire and construction sectors.[70] It is noteworthy that none of the members of the construction industry who responded to the DoE's own scrutiny report supported privatisation, while the Labour Opposition raised questions about the unfair advantage of the in-house bid team. Yet still the decision was approved a few weeks before Parliament's dissolution ahead of the general election and was justified by the outgoing minister, John Gummer, as

[67] TNA AT/66/389, John Southern, BRE Scotlab, to Tony Morris, Section Head of the FRS Building and Structures Division, 14 April 1992; GTI, FBU00000022/4, FBU Written submission, 12 March 2022.

[68] *The Times*, 26 January 1995, 20(S).

[69] Department of Trade and Industry, *Competitiveness: Forging Ahead*, Cmd. 2867 (London: HMSO, 1995); Cabinet Office, *Better Accounting for the Taxpayer's Money: The Government's Proposals*, Cmd. 2929 (London: HMSO, 1995).

[70] R. Courtney, 'Building Research Establishment – Past, Present and Future', *Building Research & Information* 25, no. 5 (1997): 285–91.

evidence of his department's commitment to 'press forward with deregulation where appropriate and sensible'.[71]

The problem was that the decision was neither appropriate nor sensible but was a blunt political instrument. Moreover, privatisation was rushed through Parliament at a time when emerging fire risks, particularly from over-cladding, demanded greater attention in the name of public safety rather than commercial exploitation. Freed from the supposed shackles of state control, BRE was '[n]ow in a position to exploit its world-class capabilities both in the UK and internationally'. Its first move was to expand its international business and make 115 of its 677 staff redundant.[72] In other words, while it had been many decades in the making, the era of state-funded fire research had come to an end, with the British government a customer of BRE much like any other organisation. Whereas once the firefighting and research communities had been joined together through their membership of centralised policy organs – notably the CFBAC, which was disbanded in 2005 – privatisation created an irrevocable split between the fire research industry and the fire service that has materially harmed public safety.

Conclusion

Left largely unsupervised, with a conscious curtailment of the enforcement powers of public fire brigades, the construction industry was able to set its own parameters for fire research and testing from the turn of the present century. Moreover, BRE's failure to provide oversight in the testing and certification process for a variety of products – including flammable cladding panels and combustible foam insulation products used in the refurbishment of Grenfell Tower in the mid-2010s – was revealed during Phase 2 of the Grenfell Inquiry and described by housing journalist Peter Apps as 'one of the great corporate scandals of our time'.[73] Simply put, by privatising fire research, successive governments since the 1970s have diminished the level of public scrutiny that was so beneficial to public safety during the three decades that followed the Second World War and, as a result, abandoned the state's responsibility for protecting its most vulnerable civilians from fire.

[71] Hansard (Commons), 27 February 1997, 454–5; *Department of the Environment Annual Report 1997*, Cmd. 3607, iv.
[72] *The Times*, 5 June 1997, 22(S); *Construction News*, 6 February 1997.
[73] Quoted in *The Spectator*, 6 December 2020.

4. The path of least intervention in the 'great unswept corner of English housing policy': multiple-fatality fires in houses in multiple occupancy in the 1980s and 1990s

Mohammed was twenty years old on arriving in Britain from Pakistan in 1985 with his younger brothers Idrees and Ikram. His goal was to finish his studies, get a good job and support his family in Islamabad. On the night of 18 November 1987, on his way home from his part-time job, Mohammed died in the disaster at King's Cross Underground along with thirty other people when an escalator fire ripped through the station. The King's Cross fire is one of the most iconic and high-profile disasters of the 1980s and, following the publication of Sir Desmond Fennell's wide-ranging public inquiry, triggered major changes in fire safety and passenger transport. In particular, the legacy of King's Cross had a significant bearing on the micro-politics of everyday life in late twentieth- and early twenty-first-century Britain – from the banning of smoking on public transport and replacement of wooden escalators in stations to the development of plastic surgery for treating burns injuries.[1] It is not therefore the focus of this final chapter, which is concerned with the many examples of forgotten multiple-fatality fires from the same era, described by contemporaries as 'the decade of disasters'.[2] We begin with Mohammed because of what happened to his family afterwards.

In an article published two years after the fire in *Roof*, the magazine of the housing charity Shelter, Idrees describes his brother's death as 'a disaster for the family' as it split them in two, with their father returning to Islamabad to care for their younger siblings. Idrees recounts how the two remaining brothers and their mother were made temporarily homeless before they were housed by Haringey Council in privately owned 'bed-and-breakfast' accommodation, otherwise known as a bedsit, with more than 100 residents sharing two kitchens and bathrooms. Their two bedrooms were 'very small and dirty and the carpets full of fleas'; despite complaining that

---

[1] Desmond Fennell, *Investigation into the King's Cross Underground Fire*, Cmd. 499 (London: Department of Transport, 1988).
[2] Ewen and Andrews, 'Media', 259–60.

the appalling conditions made their mother sick, the owners 'did nothing' to help them. Idrees also describes how the fire bell in the property 'was always going off', which would send his mum 'into a terrible panic' as it brought back painful memories of Mohammed's death. After children set fire to bedrooms in the house, the family demanded to be rehoused; they were offered a basement room in which the windows were nailed shut – hardly reassuring for a grieving family struggling to come to terms with their traumatic loss. Despite living in such conditions, Idrees describes them as one of the 'luckier' homeless families in London as they were eventually moved into a self-contained, furnished flat run by a housing association while waiting 'for something more permanent'.[3]

While the circumstances surrounding Idrees and his family's housing situation were extraordinary, it was common for the most vulnerable people in the country – low-paid migrants, students, the elderly, survivors of domestic abuse and homeless families with young children – to live in cheap, poor-quality and unsafe accommodation during the 1980s. They also, as we will repeatedly see in this chapter, lived in a state of perpetual anxiety, waiting to be moved into better housing by a state that was unwilling or unable to help. As a consequence of government housing policies, including the sale of council housing and deregulation of the private rental market, coupled with squeezed budgets for urban local authorities, the market in 'bed and breakfasts' – which often involved sub-dividing older properties into small single-room apartments with shared amenities – was booming in central London as well as inner cities across the country throughout the decade. Many private sector landlords built lucrative 'buy-to-let' businesses profiting from the growing demand for housing and local authorities' increasing inability to supply it. As Chiara Briganti and Kathy Mezei have argued, 'living with strangers' in communal housing had a long history from at least the mid-nineteenth century, but its heyday was the decades following the end of the Second World War.[4]

A succession of reports during this period consistently identified the dangerous conditions of bedsit-style housing, which became known as houses in multiple occupancy (HMOs) from the mid-1980s. Residents, environmental health officers, firefighters and housing charities repeatedly argued that unsafe fire precautions, as a spatialised social problem specific to rental housing, were the main threat to human safety in HMOs: unenclosed staircases providing the sole means of escape, combustible partition walls, a

³ *Roof*, July 1989, 44.
⁴ Chiara Briganti and Kathy Mezei, eds., *Living with Strangers: Bedsits and Boarding Houses in Modern English Life, Literature and Film* (London: Bloomsbury, 2018).

rabbit warren of corridors with poorly fitted smoke-stopping doors, defective or non-existent fire-warning and extinguishing equipment, and a lack of useful guidance for tenants.[5] As was learned in the wake of the Grenfell fire, residents' concerns are rarely taken seriously by housing providers or governments, and the same can be said for those living in unlicensed HMOs during the 1980s and 1990s.

Yet residents found a sympathetic ear in the form of voluntary organisations – charities, law centres, tenants and consumer groups – who spoke out on behalf of the millions of people like Idrees and his mother living in unsafe housing. It is to this 'third sector' – as the voluntary and community sector became known during the twenty-first century[6] – that this chapter turns. National charities like Shelter and umbrella organisations such as the Campaign for the Homeless and Roofless (CHAR) and the Campaign for Bedsit Rights (CBR), as well as local community groups and law centres, worked tirelessly over a number of years to convince government to improve safety in bedsits, bed-and-breakfast 'hotels', lodging houses and other premises where the residual poor lived, eventually achieving reform after a long campaign. This is a story that has been replicated in recent years with 'activist communities' composed of charities, grassroots organisations, trade unions and housing campaigners serving as the fulcrum around which demands for improved safety in tower blocks have coalesced. As was the case with HMOs, it is only with sustained pressure that the 2017 proclamation that 'Grenfell changes everything' can be realised by holding the state to account for its responsibility for public safety and reversing its disastrous deregulation of fire precautions.[7]

The efforts of voluntary sector organisations and activists coincided with growing support for privatisation and deregulation within the public and private sectors. Successive governments rejected the notion, spelled out in the Conservative Party's 1983 general election manifesto that 'the State can and should do everything', and placed a renewed emphasis on the role of individuals and community groups in tackling the so-called 'dependency culture' that existed at the start of the decade.[8] The Thatcher

---

[5] Alistair Cartwright, 'Rented Worlds: Bedsits, Boarding Houses and Multiple Occupancy Homes in Postwar London, 1945–1963', University of London PhD, 2020, 58.

[6] Pete Alcock, 'Voluntary Action, New Labour and the "Third Sector"', in Matthew Hilton and James McKay, eds., *The Ages of Voluntarism: How We Got to the Big Society* (Oxford: Oxford University Press, 2011), 158–79.

[7] Fiona Cornish, '"Grenfell Changes Everything?" Activism Beyond Hope and Despair', *Critical Public Health* 31, no. 3 (20021): 293–305.

[8] N.J. Crowson, 'Introduction: The Voluntary Sector in 1980s Britain', *Contemporary British History* 25, no. 4 (2011): 491–2; 'Conservative Manifesto, 1983', Margaret Thatcher Foundation,

governments and their successors increasingly relied on the market as the main agent of economic and social change and provider of welfare services.[9] Housing policy was viewed within central government as the natural preserve of market forces and a succession of acts during the 1980s and early 1990s deregulated the rental housing sector by removing government controls over the provision, cost and regulation of housing and allowing for an enhanced role for private and voluntary providers. Eighteen years of Conservative rule, argue Peter Malpass and Alan Murie, produced 'a more fragmented housing system with more dramatic differences between tenures, between urban and rural areas, and between estates and between communities'.[10]

Despite the centralising trend in housing policy, and the general mistrust from ministers towards local authorities throughout the period, central government also failed to tackle systemic defects in HMOs until the turn of the present century. Successive fires – many but certainly not all occurring in London, which faced a growing 'crisis' in the private rental market[11] – exposed the contradictions of central government policy in insisting that local authorities had sufficient discretionary powers to enforce minimum safety while failing to provide the resources to enable them to do so. This echoes recent challenges faced by the third sector in influencing policy change at the national level post-Grenfell, as well as in exposing the systemic neglect of some local authorities towards those it had a duty of care to protect. Repeated calls by professional and voluntary bodies for state intervention within the private rental housing market were at odds with government policy, which favoured an incrementally deregulated approach that prioritised the financial interests of landlords and mortgagees over and above any responsibility for safety or security. In the end, when government occasionally acted it did so by following the path of least intervention. Landlords and building owners were expected to take responsibility for their own properties with the responsible local authority stepping in to enforce the law as a last resort, which in every case followed avoidable disasters.

<https://www.margaretthatcher.org/document/110859>, accessed 6 January 2023.

[9] N.J. Crowson, Matthew Hilton, James McKay and Herjeet Marway, 'Witness Seminar: The Voluntary Sector in 1980s Britain', *Contemporary British History* 25, no. 4 (2011): 499.

[10] Peter Malpass and Alan Murie, *Housing Policy and Practice*, 5th edition (London: Macmillan, 1999), 78.

[11] See, eg, Paul Harrison, *Inside the Inner City: Life under the Cutting Edge* (London: Penguin, 1983).

Multiple-fatality fires in HMOs

In the early hours of 18 March 1980 neighbours were woken by screams from a burning hostel in Kilburn, north London, which was run by the Catholic Order of the Missionaries of Charity, headed by Mother Teresa of Calcutta. Neighbours rushed to help the residents, all women, to safety from the three-storey terraced house. Firefighters eventually discovered the bodies of eight women on the top floor; two more later succumbed to their injuries. A month before the fire London Fire Brigade had inspected the premises and recommended various improvements, including enclosing the single staircase used for exit in the event of a fire, but these had yet to be implemented by the owners. An internal review by Brent Borough Council revealed that the nuns had been awarded a licence for ten beds the previous year, but firefighters found twenty-one occupied beds.[12]

With one exception, the victims were residents and aged between thirty and seventy years.[13] All were single, though some still used marital names; being part of a transient community to which a great deal of stigma was attached, some gave pseudonyms such as 'Peggy' or 'Rose'.[14] Most of the victims were described by members of Brent Women's Aid Group as 'battered women'; that is, they were survivors of domestic violence who had been forced into emergency accommodation and were awaiting rehousing.[15] One of the residents was later arrested for starting the fire as a grudge against the nuns. At the trial, her lawyer unsympathetically told the court that the hostel catered for 'inadequate alcoholics and those who were mentally disturbed' and considered that 'any one of these women could have started the fire'. The defendant was acquitted of all charges.[16]

The victims were part of the 'hidden homeless', marginalised by a society and government that abandoned those without a fixed abode despite the 1977 Housing (Homeless Persons) Act prioritising vulnerable women such as these for rehousing. Local authorities acted inconsistently, and sometimes

---

[12] *The Times*, 19 March 1980, 1; *Willesden and Brent Chronicle* (hereafter *WBC*), 21 March 1980, 16.

[13] One of the victims was an eighteen-year-old voluntary care worker on her first shift. Their names are listed in Shane Ewen, 'The Tragedy of the Hidden Homeless: Living in Death-Trap Hostels in Thatcher's Britain', *Fire Brigades Union Blog*, 18 March 2020, <https://www.fbu.org.uk/blog/tragedy-hidden-homeless-living-death-trap-hostels -thatchers-britain>.

[14] *Daily Express*, 19 March 1980, 1, 3.

[15] *WBC*, 28 March 1980, 2, 18.

[16] *The Times*, 18 December 1980, 3.

indiscriminately, in prioritising families at the expense of single persons.[17] They also suffered from cuts in government subsidy which forced poor boroughs like Brent to close their housing priority lists because of over-subscription. Single older women thus faced limited housing options and many were forced into direct-access hostels even though these were disliked: 'I couldn't bear to live in one of those places – it would make me feel I'd reached the end of the road, with nowhere further to go', claimed one woman interviewed for a contemporary study.[18] A spokesperson for Brent Women's Centre reported that public expenditure restrictions made it 'much more difficult for women and children to escape from violent homes by finding a place of their own'.[19]

The Kilburn fire horrifically exposed the need for action in what had become a crisis in the safety of emergency accommodation for society's most vulnerable citizens. It was the latest in a growing number of fires since the late 1970s: in 1978 alone, thirteen people died in hostel blazes across the country, including in Birmingham, Leeds and Clacton.[20] The night after the Kilburn fire, seven people were rescued from a fire in a mission hostel in east London. A spokesperson for CHAR, a parliamentary lobby coalition, said, 'It is appalling that there are second-class standards for people regarded as second-class citizens.'[21]

These fires occurred against a backdrop of major changes to housing policy from the recently elected Conservative Government. By giving council house tenants the 'Right to Buy' their homes, Thatcher's flagship housing bill revived the party's longstanding commitment to building a property-owning democracy through introducing greater choice in housing ownership and limiting the responsibilities of the state.[22] While benefiting those in a position to purchase their home on generous terms, it was not lost on Brent councillors that such a move would do nothing to help those who dreamt of living in a council house; in fact, by limiting the supply of houses, government narrowed the already slim options open to the

---

[17] Val Binney, Gina Harkell and Judy Nixon, *Leaving Violent Men: A Study of Refuges and Housing for Battered Women* (London: Women's Aid Federation, 1982); Nicholas J. Crowson, 'Revisiting the 1977 Housing (Homeless Persons) Act: Westminster, Whitehall, and the Homelessness Lobby', *Twentieth Century British History* 24, no. 3 (2012): 424–47.

[18] Sophie Watson and Helen Austerberry, *Housing and Homelessness: A Feminist Perspective* (London: Routledge, 1986), 160.

[19] *WBC*, 4 January 1980, 3; 28 November 1980, 7.

[20] *CHAR Report* (London: Campaign for the Homeless and Roofless, 1982), 17–18.

[21] *Daily Mirror*, 20 March 1980, 11.

[22] Aled Davies, '"Right to Buy": The Development of a Conservative Housing Policy, 1945–1980', *Contemporary British History* 27, no. 4 (2013): 421–44.

---

most vulnerable people living in one of London's 'worst areas of housing deprivation', according to a report published later that year.[23] In mid-1980, Brent Council housed 220 families in bed-and-breakfast accommodation in neighbouring boroughs at a cost of over £100 each per week.[24] Moreover, 'drastic cuts' to its budget meant that the council was unable to improve its existing housing stock, with the leader of the local Labour group blaming central government: 'We even made a special plea to Government to allow us extra money to at least carry out fire precaution works ... but no help was forthcoming.'[25] The council's review recommended bringing the regulation of hostels in line with the law on hotels and boarding houses, introducing enforcement powers to close down premises 'where there is excessive risk to persons'.[26]

For a fleeting moment, the 'hidden homeless' became visible to a government whose own housing minister had described hostels as 'the great unswept corner of English housing policy'.[27] Spurred into action by pressure from religious leaders and homelessness charities, government agreed to amend its housing bill to strengthen local authority powers for dealing with large HMOs.[28] But it rejected extending the Fire Precautions Act to cover hostels, with the home secretary, William Whitelaw, explaining that they 'do not represent a risk to life serious enough to justify the burden which would be imposed on owners, occupiers and fire authorities'.[29] The government's own evidence did not support this hard line since official statistics collected by the Home Office revealed the risk of a fire in an HMO to be three or four times higher than in a single-occupancy house, while the risk of serious injury or death was nine or ten times greater.[30]

A few months later, the jury for the inquest into the Kilburn victims returned a verdict of unlawful killing and called for urgent clarification of the law on means of escape. Noting the brief period in which a policy window opens following multiple-fatality fires, the coroner Dr David Paul complained that 'the spur and urgency of this newsworthy tragedy lost its impetus' amidst the cumbersome procedure of government review

[23] *WBC*, 17 October 1980, 1; 24 October 1980, 14.
[24] *WBC*, 22 August 1980, 3.
[25] *WBC*, 24 October 1980, 3.
[26] *WBC*, 25 April 1980, 1, 18.
[27] Hansard (Commons), 25 February 1983, 1142.
[28] Hansard (Commons), 6 August 1980, 684–7.
[29] *WBC*, 26 December 1980, 3.
[30] TNA AT/49/116, 'Application of Building Regulations to Houses in Multiple Occupation'.

and obfuscation.[31] The fact that few newspapers even bothered to report on the verdict substantiates his point and shows how little national media interest was shown in the lives of 'battered women'. It also resonates with comments made by Sam Webb about his memories of the Ronan Point inquiry, which, owing to the fact that 'it took an hour and a half to get to East Ham from ... central London', attracted little attention from the national press 'after the first few days'.[32]

Ignoring the coroner's criticism, government opted to take the path of least intervention. A duty was placed on local housing authorities requiring means of escape from fire in large HMOs of three storeys or more and with a combined floor space exceeding 500 square metres.[33] Guidance would clarify the law on means of escape in other HMOs, eventually being published several years later.[34] The decision to devolve responsibility to housing authorities seems to have been influenced by party-political antagonisms in London where the Labour Party had recently taken control of the Greater London Council (GLC), which had responsibility for the London Fire Brigade, as well as a general resistance to arming fire brigades with additional powers given they were regarded as being tougher in enforcing fire precautions. While the Order was welcomed by campaigners as 'a long overdue safeguard', it was also noted that less than 2 per cent of all HMOs were covered by the law and that only 1 per cent of all improvement grants went towards the provision of fire escapes. With a gross floor space of only 226 square metres, the Kilburn hostel was too small to be included, making 'a mockery of the new duty', claimed the director of CHAR Nicholas Beacock, who predicted 'further tragedies' before the law was properly updated.[35]

And so it proved. In December 1981, fire gutted a large property on Clanricarde Gardens in west London, killing eight residents and injuring many more. Notting Hill Gate was an area notorious for cheap, low-quality housing and illegal landlord practices: the 'slumlord' Peter Rachman had operated in the neighbourhood during the 1960s and little had improved, judging from this latest disaster. The properties comprised fifty-six bedsits across three converted Victorian terraced houses. The figures on occupancy

[31] *WBC*, 30 January 1981, 4.

[32] ESCH 2018_esch_RoPo_04, Interview with Webb.

[33] The Housing (Means of Escape from Fire in Houses in Multiple Occupation) Order 1981. S.I. 1981/1576.

[34] Hansard (Commons), 17 December 1980, 174W; 4 February 1981, 114W.

[35] *CHAR Report* (London: Campaign for the Homeless and Roofless, 1981), 18–19; TNA AT/49/116, The Houses in Multiple Occupation Group, Briefing Paper, 24 October 1983.

ranged widely: whereas the landlord incorrectly claimed that only fifty-three tenants resided on the premises, first responders estimated between 150 and 200 persons in occupancy on the night of the fire. The housekeeper, who lived on the ground floor, later confirmed the figure to be ninety-three residents, the majority of whom were low-paid migrant workers and the elderly. By lunchtime, all the refugees from the fire, some dressed in their nightclothes with their belongings wrapped in bedsheets, were given shelter, with food and clothing generously donated by market traders. The local authority, Kensington and Chelsea London Borough Council (KCLBC), provided temporary accommodation in hotels, from where its staff interviewed survivors to determine which families should be given priority for rehousing before Christmas. The bleak prospects for rehousing led to twenty-five tenants accepting accommodation owned by the same landlord, with some even moving into the house next to the burnt-out shell that remained.[36]

In the aftermath of the fire, the attention of voluntary and community groups turned to the poor standard of safety within the property and the fears of residents living in similar accommodation across the borough. Kensington and Chelsea was described as having 'some of the poorest housing conditions in the country', with HMOs comprising between a quarter and a third of its housing stock. A survey by a local race and housing action group revealed that the borough also had the highest rents among its council housing stock and the lowest average rate of pay in the capital.[37] It was also claimed that KCLBC had not acted upon residents' complaints about safety six months before the fire. One report, compiled by an environmental health consultant on behalf of Shelter and the North Kensington Law Centre (NKLC), concluded that 'the arrangements to limit the spread of fire and secure the safe evacuation of occupants are inadequate'. After it was further revealed that KCLBC maintained no register of HMOs within the borough, the leader of the Labour Opposition demanded an internal inquiry into 'what went wrong'. KCLBC was later found guilty of maladministration by the local government ombudsman and in direct contravention of race relations legislation, having 'failed to follow up complaints over a number of years'.[38]

Fire investigation officers discovered a litany of safety defects, including combustible partition walls, unprotected staircases and a dangerously high electrical loading. At the inquest at Westminster Coroners Court, an

[36] *Kensington News & Post* (hereafter *KNP*), 18 December 1981, 1, 3; 25 December 1981, 1.
[37] *Roof*, March 1989, 10.
[38] *KNP*, 25 December 1981, 3; 29 January 1982, 3.

'independent' expert, Keith Gugan, who was acting on behalf of the insurers and landlord, claimed that the fire had been maliciously started by a tenant, which attracted greater media interest than the identities of the victims.[39] Gugan's findings were challenged by experts appearing on behalf of London Fire Brigade and the Metropolitan Police and the coroner, Dr Paul Knapman, rebuked him for failing to produce forensic evidence to substantiate his claim. The landlord was called to give evidence but refused to answer questions.[40]

The main issue, according to counsel acting for the bereaved families, was that the fire had broken out in 'slums without the most elementary fire protection', which demonstrated 'reckless' negligence by the landlord and warranted a verdict of unlawful killing. Knapman replied that the job of an inquest was 'to find out where, when and how a person met their death – not to apportion blame'.[41] After nine days, the jury returned a verdict of death by misadventure, finding no evidence of negligence. Furthermore, Knapman declined to add recommendations on safety to the verdict, claiming that the need to reconcile cheap accommodation for homeless people with 'expensive' fire precautions was an 'insoluble problem'. This decision angered campaigners. Michael O'Dwyer, who represented bereaved families for the NKLC, called the decision an 'outrage' and criticised Knapman for failing the victims, before adding: 'We will go on pressing for more resources, for better fire precautions to be introduced into houses in multiple occupation and for landlords to own up to their responsibilities – we will not stop until we reach that.[42] Survivors were still pursuing a claim for damages several years later.

This case illustrates the limited opportunities facing survivors and the bereaved in having their voices heard in formal judicial settings. As the first neighbourhood law centre in the country, opened in 1970 in a former butcher's shop, NKLC operated on the premise that lawyers failed to act in the interests of those communities in greatest need of help. NKLC provided free legal advice and representation to those who could not otherwise afford it for a range of issues including immigration law and housing rights; they also assisted with claims for compensation following fire inquests. Law centres thus amplified the voices of those communities most directly affected by avoidable multiple-fatality fires, allowing them to seek justice and obtain some closure to a horrific chapter in their lives. But the law centres were also in a parlous situation, as Kate Bradley has shown:

[39] *Daily Express*, 19 December 1981, 5; *Daily Mirror*, 3 March 1982, 15.
[40] *KNP*, 5 March 1982, 1.
[41] *KNP*, 12 March 1982, 1–3.
[42] *KNP*, 19 March 1982, 8.

they experienced problems with securing a regular income, struggled with under-staffing and were often accused of being politically motivated in their casework. Some were threatened with losing their main funding stream when they openly criticised local authority policies.[43]

Following the Clanricarde Gardens verdict, the government declined to strengthen the law or give serious consideration to practical solutions. When the Institute of Environmental Health Officers and CHAR jointly submitted a proposal for national licensing, the undersecretary of state for the environment, George Young, expressed 'serious reservations about the cost implications of such proposals at a time when the Government is concerned to see restraint in local authority expenditure'.[44] While the proposal was costed to be self-financing, it would have entailed transferring funds from the Department of Health and Social Security budget to local authority housing departments, which was contrary to Whitehall policy to 'trim' local government spending. Moreover, Young warned that licensing 'would add unnecessarily to landlord's cost [sic], and discourage them from making accommodation available', which prompted some to question whether many Conservative MPs were themselves owners of HMOs: 'there could be some very red faces at Westminster', suggested one journalist writing for *The Surveyor*, though such lines of enquiry never appeared in the popular press.[45]

Although housing charities found themselves frozen out of decision making by a government that was hostile towards single-issue campaigning, they found support among opposition parties as well as the Tory backbenches. Frustrated by government's 'neglect and inaction', in 1983 Labour MP Jim Marshall's private bill proposed to introduce a duty on local authorities to ensure proper means of escape in all HMOs. Brandon Rhys-Williams, Conservative MP for North Kensington, the constituency in which the fire at Clanricarde Gardens occurred, supported the bill and warned that it was incumbent on Parliament to not allow 'that horror to be repeated'.[46] His warnings were echoed by John Wheeler, Conservative MP for neighbouring Paddington: 'It is a scandal that people should lose their lives for the lack of a determination in the House [of Commons] to ensure that the law provides the protection that they need.'[47] Only with effective and enforceable

[43] Kate Bradley, *Lawyers for the Poor: Legal Advice, Voluntary Action and Citizenship in England, 1890–1990* (Manchester: Manchester University Press, 2019), 162–8.
[44] *The Surveyor*, 11 October 1984, 27, in TNA AT/49/116, 'Application of Building Regulations to Houses in Multiple Occupation'.
[45] *The Surveyor*.
[46] Hansard (Commons), 25 February 1983, 1175.
[47] Hansard (Commons), 25 February 1983, 1182.

regulations would lives be saved in future, claimed Labour MP for Swansea East Donald Anderson, who added that this would be 'the best memorial that the House could give to those who died at Clanricarde Gardens'.[48]

Despite passing its second reading in February 1983, the bill was dropped after Parliament's dissolution ahead of the general election and it was not adopted as part of the new government's legislative agenda. Low rates of house-building for rent, coupled with the acceleration of the sale of council homes, led to an increase in homelessness in the mid-1980s in metropolitan areas. Homeless people had little option but to live in substandard accommodation, while local authorities struggled to provide a satisfactory alternative for single-person households. Chris Holmes, the director of CHAR and one of the draftees of the bill, calculated that the number of claimants in bed-and-breakfast accommodation in England and Wales increased fourfold from 25,000 to 100,000 between 1979 and 1984. Research showed that 81 per cent of those living in HMOs were single, 35 per cent of whom were women and 65 per cent under the age of thirty-five. The 'worsening crisis of single homelessness', Holmes argued, demanded three urgent and interlinked actions by the state in order to provide 'a safe, secure and satisfactory home for every member of the community': additional social rented housing, security of tenure and the enforcement of minimum standards of fire safety, amenities and management of HMOs.[49]

In 1985, a consolidating act made tentative steps towards improving standards but disappointed campaigners who expected quicker progress. This followed the death of a Bangladeshi mother and her children in a five-storey bed-and-breakfast fire in Gloucester Place, Westminster, which finally prompted Dr Knapman to write to ministers urging that 'action be taken to prevent the occurrence of similar fatalities'.[50] This fire exposed the racial inequalities in London's rental housing market, with this particular 'halfway house' grossly overcrowded with Asian families who should have been priority cases for rehousing; the family had lived in a single room at the top of an unenclosed staircase for the past nine months, while firefighters

[48] Hansard (Commons), 5 May 1983, 532.

[49] Malpass and Murie, *Housing Policy and Practice*, 243; Chris Holmes, 'The Worsening Crisis of Single Homelessness', in Peter Malpass, ed., *The Housing Crisis* (London: Croom Helm, 1986), 200–14.

[50] *Roof*, January 1987, 6. A similar urgency for action was expressed by Assistant Deputy Coroner Frances Kirkham to Secretary of State for Communities and Local Government Eric Pickles following an inquest into the six deaths at the 2009 Lakanal House fire, 28 March 2013, at <https://www.lambeth.gov.uk/sites/default/files/ec-letter-to-DCLG-pursuant-to-rule43-28March2013.pdf>. Pickles's reply, 20 May 2013, is at GTI, HOM00048299/3, 29 March 2022.

found as many as seven people sleeping to a room and rescued a baby sleeping in a cot in a bathroom.[51] The inquest again revealed 'totally and hopelessly inadequate' fire precautions, including a wooden ladder used in lieu of an escape, but the landlord – who had received £356,000 in rent to house homeless families from neighbouring Camden – ignored warnings from frightened tenants. One resident reported that he had tried to fight the fire but all the extinguishers in the house were empty.[52]

Survivors from the fire decided that direct action was the route to escaping the squalor of halfway houses. Assisted by the Camden Committee for Community Relations, a local pressure group funded by the borough council, up to seventy homeless people, many with young children, organised a three-week occupation of Camden Town Hall until the Labour group agreed to permanently rehouse them in council houses. Two heavily pregnant women slept on the chamber floor for over a week, deeming it preferable to staying in their death-trap bedsits.[53] While local press coverage was consistently detailed, national media interest was virtually non-existent, with few newspapers reporting on either the fire or the town hall's occupation. Eventually, the novelist Salman Rushdie wrote an excoriating piece for *The Guardian* in which he argued that Black and Asian families, who made up between a third and half of all families living in London's halfway houses, were being victimised by racist slumlords and councillors. With evidence emerging that the fire was started deliberately, Rushdie likened it to the 1981 New Cross Massacre, in which thirteen young Black men, women and children died in a suspected racist attack on a house party, but in neither case did the Metropolitan Police pursue the cases seriously. 'Presumably not enough people have been burned to death yet', Rushdie wrote before demanding that 'it is time people stopped having to die to prove to local authorities that they live in hideously unsatisfactory conditions'.[54]

Despite the best efforts of campaigners to raise the plight of homeless families, ministers did the bare minimum. Firstly, an HMO was defined as 'a house which is occupied by persons who do not form a single household', creating more legal ambiguities than it solved. Secondly, local authorities were awarded discretionary powers to establish registration schemes in their

[51] *The Standard*, 21 November 1984, 2.
[52] *Camden New Journal*, 27 June 1985, 1, 13, 18.
[53] *Camden New Journal*, 29 November–20 December 1984.
[54] *The Guardian*, 3 December 1984, 12; Aaron Andrews, 'Truth, Justice, and Expertise in 1980s Britain: The Cultural Politics of the New Cross Massacre', *History Workshop Journal* 91, no. 1 (2021): 182–209. Two-and-a-half years after the New Cross fire, a young male took his own life, becoming the fourteenth victim of the massacre.

area, but few took advantage of these. Thirdly, a 'fitness' test was drawn up for governing HMOs, which provided for regulations to render premises fit for occupants, covering areas ranging from lighting and ventilation to space-heating appliances.[55] Despite calls to establish means of escape in the event of a fire as a condition of fitness, this was not originally included despite a government-commissioned survey unearthing 'disturbing' evidence that 81 per cent of HMOs lacked satisfactory means of escape; the figure rose above 90 per cent for privately owned properties. In Greater London, where 43 per cent of all HMOs in England and Wales were located, over 80 per cent had defective means of escape, while 'a substantial minority' of larger HMOs continued to lack precautions. This 'hidden housing problem' was now so visible to policymakers that it could no longer be ignored by ministers.[56] But ignore it they did. While the recast Building Regulations specified mandatory rules for means of escape in case of fire for dwellings and flats of three or more storeys, these did not originally extend to HMOs, though guidance on fire safety was issued in 1986, four years after it was initially promised, and an advisory standard was adopted two years later.[57]

In the intervening period, a revised private members' bill was promoted by opposition MPs, which included prescriptive measures to tackle what had become 'a national scandal'. Its timing was bad, being promoted during the period of 'high Thatcherism' when central government curbed the powers of local authorities through rate capping and the abolition of the GLC and metropolitan councils. Indeed, the government, having failed to block the bill's debate, disrespectfully sent its minister for sport, Richard Tracey, to present the case that legislation was not required and the bill was timed out through filibustering by backbench Tory MPs.[58]

Despite their understandable frustration at the government's intransigence towards housing provision for the poor, homelessness charities learned a great deal about campaigning during the 1980s. One such group was CBR, founded by Nick Beacock following the fire at Clanricarde Gardens.[59] As a former director of CHAR who had been active in the writing of homelessness

---

[55] Housing Act, 1985, sections 345, 352, 365.

[56] Andrew Thomas and A. Hedges, *The 1985 Physical and Social Survey of Houses in Multiple Occupation in England and Wales* (London: HMSO, 1986), 23–4.

[57] Department of the Environment, *The Building Regulations: Mandatory Rules for Means of Escape in Case of Fire* (London: HMSO, 1985); Department of the Environment, *Guide to Means of Escape and Related Fire Safety Measures in Certain Existing Houses in Multiple Occupation* (London: HMSO, 1988).

[58] Hansard (Commons), 13 February 1987, 610–38; Ben Jackson and Robert Saunders, 'Varieties of Thatcherism', in Jackson and Saunders, *Thatcher's Britain*, 7.

[59] CBR became a specialist unit within Shelter in 1997.

legislation in the 1970s, Beacock enjoyed good contacts across Parliament and with sympathetic newspapers, using these to advocate for an evidence-based approach to policymaking. As Matthew Hilton et al. have shown, the importance of a professional media strategy was increasingly apparent to non-governmental organisations by the 1980s in order to react swiftly to any item in the news and to offer journalists an alternative interpretation on policies.[60] Beacock was no stranger to this approach: CBR's small staff were regular correspondents with broadsheet newspapers and repeatedly quoted in press coverage of bedsit fires and related topics.[61] Although the CBR team's efforts to secure media coverage met resistance from some popular daily newspapers – in 1990 the *Evening Standard* and *Daily Mail* both cited CBR as a recipient of 'daft donations' by 'loony left' councils – it operated a sustained campaign on a shoestring budget, receiving grants from the London Boroughs Grants Committee as well as member subscriptions.[62]

In addition to its media campaigning, CBR also published handbooks aimed at tenants in an attempt to directly improve the standard of housing in HMOs. These handbooks contained advice and useful contacts about tenants' legal rights and landlords' duty of care, as well as fire safety hints and tips. Owing to CBR's parlous financial arrangements, these publications were generously supported by other voluntary and professional bodies. Organisations such as the Law Society, Crisis, the National Association of Citizens Advice Bureaux, Fire Brigades Union (FBU) and the Housing Associations Charitable Trust helped to lend CBR a more authoritative voice, illustrating the importance of cross-sectoral groups coming together to form 'activist communities' to deal with the problem in the absence of leadership from central or local government.[63]

At a time when single-issue groups struggled to exert influence within central government, CBR raised standards of safety locally through a dense network of tenants' groups, local authorities, student unions, law centres and other organisations. Grassroots campaigning enjoyed success in cities with progressive councils, such as Birmingham, Bristol and Southampton, using

---

[60] Matthew Hilton, James McKay, Nicholas Crowson and Jean-François Mouhot, *The Politics of Expertise: How NGOs Shaped Modern Britain* (Oxford: Oxford University Press, 2013), 154–7.

[61] *The Standard*, 22 January 1985, 16; *The Guardian*, 11 April 1988, 18; *Evening Standard*, 20 August 1993, 14.

[62] *Evening Standard*, 20 March 1990, 2; *Daily Mail*, 25 April 1990, 9.

[63] Campaign for Bedsit Rights, *Bedsit Rights: A Handbook for People Who Live in Bedsits* (London: CHAR, 1989); Roger Critchley, *Fire Safety Guide* (London: Campaign for Bedsit Rights, 1991).

a mixture of activist strategies to improve housing conditions.[64] In Wales, a cross-sectoral approach was agreed following the death of a man in a fire at a Pontypridd hostel in 1986, while the all-party Welsh Affairs Committee unanimously supported urgent legislation.[65] Direct action demonstrated that the best route to positive change was from below. Private tenants' organisations such as the Brent Private Tenants Rights Group, Kensington & Chelsea Private Tenants Rights Project and the Camden Federation of Private Tenants – the latter formed in the aftermath of the successful occupation of Camden Town Hall – built on deep-rooted grassroots activism that dated from the late 1960s, while the effectiveness of the Welsh campaign pointed to what could be achieved with a progressive government in Whitehall.[66]

Licensing HMOs

While the Thatcher Government stubbornly refused to intervene to protect the safety of those who most needed protecting, the fatalities continued to occur. In the five years to 1991, an average of 168 people a year died and 3,294 were injured in HMO fires according to the government's own published statistics. One fire in 1988, in a Blackpool hostel, resulted in the deaths of three children and two adults from the same family. The premises were used by the Department of Social Security (DSS) to house unemployed families. Newspapers reported that children smashed windows and climbed onto ledges to escape the choking smoke.[67] Shortly afterwards, a flimsy ten-page consultation paper rejected licensing and even had the temerity to recommend redefining HMOs, which would have halved the number protected by existing safeguards. Even the Conservative-controlled Association of District Councils, a staunch advocate of a tougher stance on local authority finances, criticised the report for contradicting the government's own evidence.[68]

Instead, government passed the Housing and Local Government Act 1989, which aimed to revive the private rental sector through deregulation while continuing the erosion of local authority provision through new financial arrangements for housing associations. The introduction of shorthold tenancies gave landlords greater controls over properties, including powers to

[64] *Bedsit Briefing*, August 1987, 4, 7; November 1987, 2–3; *Roof*, January 1995, 34–5.

[65] *Bedsit Rights*, spring 1987; August 1987, 5; *Bedsit Briefing*, June 1987, 5.

[66] Peter Shapely, 'Tenants Arise! Consumerism, Tenants and the Challenge to Council Authority in Manchester, 1968–92', *Social History* 31, no. 1 (2006): 60–78.

[67] *Daily Mirror*, 6 April 1988, 2; *The Times*, 6 April 1988, 1, 20.

[68] Department of the Environment, *Consultation Paper on Houses in Multiple Occupation* (London: HMSO, 1988); *The Challenges of Multiple Occupancy: A Fresh Look at HMOs* (London: Association of District Councils, 1988).

gain possession through eviction notices, either to re-let them on high-rent-assured tenancies or to convert them for sale.[69] The promise of a substantial profit from a quick sale – property speculation was rife in Kensington and Chelsea in the late 1980s, for instance, with a pair of vacant properties on Clanricarde Gardens valued at £1.4 million (nearly £4 million according to 2020 prices) – was a powerful incentive for landlords to 'persuade' tenants to leave through low-level harassment at the same time that many local authorities cut their housing support services.[70]

Fire by fire, the campaigners chipped away at policymakers. In 1991, a damning report issued by the National Consumer Council (NCC) described HMOs as 'deathtrap housing' and repeated calls for mandatory licensing. Given the 'Right to Buy' programme had been framed in terms of giving greater choice to consumer-citizens, so too should the same rights of consumer protection be extended to poorly housed renters. In her foreword to the report, Lady Wilcox, the NCC chair, wrote, 'Most of us associate deathtrap housing with the squalid slums of our Dickensian past. But this report shows that even today millions of people are renting dangerous housing, often without knowing the dangers until things go wrong.'[71] With the widening of the campaign beyond the homelessness charities, it was finally reaching its desired audience as well as attracting sympathetic press attention: while charges for registration schemes had already been introduced earlier in the year, advisory guidance on standards of fitness followed a year later.[72] This left one significant obstacle for campaigners to overcome: deregulation.

In 1993, John Major's Conservative Government launched its Deregulation Task Force to review a raft of regulations dealing with health and safety legislation. The review of fire safety recommended repealing fire precautions legislation and transferring responsibility for oversight to the Health and Safety Executive. The goal was to engender a cultural shift within the fire service away from a prescriptive approach to a risk-based one where self-compliance predominated. An internal review supported repeal and also rejected licensing HMOs on the grounds that it would 'run counter to the Government's deregulation initiative'.[73] In its response, the FBU

[69] Malpass and Murie, *Housing Policy and Practice*, 83–4.

[70] *Roof,* March 1989, 10.

[71] *Deathtrap Housing: Tackling Fire Hazards for Tenants of Houses in Multiple Occupation* (London: National Consumer Council, 1991).

[72] *Daily Mail*, 26 September 1991, 12; *The Times*, 26 September 1991, 2; Department of the Environment, *Houses in Multiple Occupation: Guidance to Local Housing Authorities on Standards of Fitness under Section 352 of the Housing Act 1985* (London: HMSO, 1992).

[73] P.R. Edmundson and G.I. Hubbard, *A Review of the Fire Precautions Act 1971* (London: Home Office, 1993), 48–9.

warned that repealing legislation would 'give entirely the wrong signals and could be misinterpreted as a move to lower standards of fire safety'. Instead, the FBU argued for the extension of inspection and certification to HMOs and other higher-risk premises.[74] But the decision was a *fait accompli*: deregulation, claimed Home Secretary Michael Howard, would improve public safety by constituting 'an approach which places the responsibility for assessing risks, and dealing with them, on those who create the risks'.[75] Government remained committed to a path of least intervention, having seemingly learned little from past failures to mitigate against mass fatalities.

Failure to learn was brutally exposed in May 1994 when an adult female and two-year-old child died in another coastal resort fire, this time at a Scarborough hostel for DSS claimants; it was subsequently discovered that the owner had failed to comply with an order to upgrade the premises' means of escape.[76] Later that day, Major committed his government to 'investigating the feasibility of introducing a licensing system to control such establishments'.[77] While the subsequent consultation paper accepted that there were strong arguments in favour of licensing (76 per cent of respondents favoured mandatory registration), it also warned that, following the deregulation of the private rental market, 'it would be introducing too high a degree of licensing', which could lead either to tenants being charged higher rents to pay for the improvements or landlords withdrawing from the market.[78] Ministers concluded that 'a full-scale national and mandatory licensing system cannot be justified' on the grounds that 'it would lead to excessive cost and bureaucracy by forcing every local authority to follow a standard licensing approach'.[79] The 1996 Housing Act thus imposed a broad duty of care on landlords in respect of safety and other amenity standards, while also allowing the secretary of state to make model registration schemes for adoption by local authorities.[80] Following almost two decades

---

[74] Fire Brigades Union, *Who Will Pick Up the Pieces? Response to the Government's Interdepartmental Review of Fire Safety Legislation and Enforcement* (Kingston upon Thames: Fire Brigades Union, 1994), 39, 56.

[75] *Fire*, November 1994, 22.

[76] *The Times*, 6 May 1994, 3.

[77] Hansard (Commons), 5 May 1994, 841.

[78] Department of the Environment, *Houses in Multiple Occupation: Consultation Paper on the Case for Licensing* (London: HMSO, 1994), 6.

[79] Department of the Environment, *Improving Standards in Houses in Multiple Occupation* (London: HMSO, 1995), 3.

[80] Nicholas J. Smith, 'Bureaucracy or Death: Safeguarding Lives in Houses in Multiple Occupation', in David Cowan, ed., *Housing: Participation and Exclusion* (London: Routledge, 1998), 168–88.

of campaigning, multiple reviews and consultations, legal confusion and hundreds of avoidable deaths, the country was on the verge of a national system of licensing if only a government had the gumption to enact it.

According to Jane Lewis and Pete Alcock, a change in government in 1997 heralded a new era of voluntary action favouring 'partnership working' between the state and the third sector.[81] Taking its cue from the operation of successful local schemes, the incumbent New Labour Government pledged to resolve the fire safety problem through 'a proper system of licensing for local authorities which will benefit tenants and responsible landlords alike'.[82] The following year, government-commissioned research underpinned proposals for a new code of practice and recommended that the best approach to reducing fire deaths was education coupled with enforcement. As befitted the era, an emphasis was placed on collaborative working across the public, private and third sectors to mitigate the risks. Charities like Shelter and Crisis were consequently brought into the fold to help devise national policy.[83] While New Labour completed its predecessor's policy to increase self-compliance measures, it also recognised that HMOs were 'a special case' demanding 'better regulation'.[84]

Taking a further six years to get onto the statute books, the Housing Act 2004 finally introduced compulsory licensing for HMOs, the definition of which was widened to include a house of three or more storeys occupied by five or more unrelated persons and sharing basic amenities. This brought a large number of unprotected premises under the law, including house shares of groups of students and young professionals. Landlords would be screened by housing officers, following consultation with fire authorities, to determine whether they were 'a fit and proper person' suitable for letting property. Welcomed by many in the third sector as an effective way of protecting public safety, critics resorted to kneejerk arguments that 'buy-to-let' investors were being 'smothered in red tape' which would result in 'the better landlords' deciding that 'it is just not worth the hassle' to continue in the rental market. 'It's such a hard life being a landlord', bemoaned one writer in a particularly egregious piece published by *The Times* on behalf of the

---

[81] Jane Lewis, 'New Labour's Approach to the Voluntary Sector: Independence and the Meaning of Partnership', *Social Policy & Society* 4, no. 2 (2005): 121–31; Alcock, 'Voluntary Action', 173–7.

[82] *1997 Labour Party Manifesto*, <http://www.labour-party.org.uk/manifestos/1997/1997 -labour-manifesto.shtml>, accessed 6 January 2023.

[83] Christopher Holmes, *A New Vision for Housing* (London: Routledge, 2006).

[84] Home Office, *Fire Safety Legislation for the Future: A Consultation Document* (London: HMSO, 1997), 24; Department of Environment, Trade and the Regions, *Licensing of Houses in Multiple Occupation – England* (London: HMSO, 1999).

National Landlords Association, which was more concerned at the impact licensing could have on investors' returns than the safety of residents.[85] If a reminder was needed that Whitehall had finally intervened to protect the lives of those least able to protect themselves, this came in the form of a hostel fire in Birmingham, which caused the deaths of four residents. This fire provided further proof of the importance of multi-agency partnerships to protect 'vulnerable tenants' against negligent landlords, many of whom openly 'flout legislation'.[86] The battle to sweep the great unswept corner of English housing policy was a long one and it would require periodic cleaning to deal with stubborn stains.

Conclusion

This chapter echoes Nicholas Crowson's contention that the voluntary sector was at the heart of the 'mixed economy' of welfare reform during the 1980s and continued to play a central role as part of a widened 'third sector' during the 1990s and 2000s. Homelessness charities, law centres and community groups were a continuous source of support for residents and a thorn in the side of governments, holding the latter to account for their reluctance to regulate safety in the private rental housing sector. More importantly, in advocating on behalf of the groups most vulnerable to fire, including victims, survivors and bereaved and grief-stricken families, voluntary and community groups spoke on behalf of the people and communities who otherwise received scant representation within mainstream political, legal or media discourse around housing. They interposed themselves between an indifferent, occasionally hostile, executive on the one side and Parliament on the other, while also creating dense networks of grassroots activists who raised safety standards from the bottom up, often in collaboration with environmental safety and fire prevention officers as well as trade unions. What campaigners lacked in terms of direct influence over policymakers at the heart of government, who generally favoured a 'top-down' approach to policy 'unencumbered by the constraints provided by interest groups', they more than made up for in perseverance and partnership-building at both the local and national levels of civil society.[87]

The lessons here for third-sector organisations to work in partnership in the wake of the Grenfell Tower fire offer a glimmer of hope for activists and safety campaigners determined to effect lasting cultural and regulatory changes to building safety. That they will have to continue fighting for

---

[85] *The Times*, 6 May 2005, 'Bricks and Mortar' section, 16.
[86] *Fire*, April 2005, 22–3.
[87] Crowson, 'Introduction', 491, 496.

justice and reform after the publication of the final report into the public inquiry is testament to the courage and resilience of those who have been most directly affected by the events of 14 June 2017 and the consequent 'cladding crisis' that has eroded public faith in government's moral purpose to provide security for its citizens. Having been brought into the fold to deal with the problem of HMOs at the turn of the present century, 'activist communities' find themselves at a similar crossroads in 2023 as we head towards a forthcoming general election in which trust in our democratically elected representatives will be tested.

Returning to this chapter's opening example, the thirty-one victims of the 1987 King's Cross fire are remembered through regular memorial services on significant anniversaries. These have been held at St Pancras New Church (where a plaque was erected by the trustees of the disaster fund) as well as in the station concourse, where a memorial site comprising two plaques and a commemorative clock has evolved as part of its refurbishment.[88] This site serves as a reminder of those who lost their lives to anyone who seeks it out, as I do whenever I travel to London. It also offers reassurance and comfort to many of the families affected by the tragedy, as Mohammed's younger sister, Anila, who was thirteen at the time of the fire, described following the thirtieth anniversary memorial service in 2017: 'I feel like I am among my own family here … Whenever I pass through the station I always stop at this spot and touch his name on the memorial, but today there is something special about being among the other families and supporting each other.'[89] In addition to the memorial providing a space for remembrance, the legacy of the official independent inquiry, headed by the high court judge Desmond Fennell QC, also served to underline that lessons were learned and acted upon by government. Statutorily improved standards of health and safety on the Underground network are a lasting memorial to the thirty-one victims that we all benefit from whenever we travel on the Tube and whether we pause at the memorial or not as we go about our daily lives.

Unfortunately, the same cannot be said of the many victims of fires in HMOs. To my knowledge, none of these fires has ever been commemorated with a formal plaque or a memorial service. As the properties have long since

[88] BBC News, 17 November 2007, <http://news.bbc.co.uk/1/hi/england/london/7099677.stm>. Colin Townsley's sacrifice has also been remembered through the erection of a Red Plaque outside the premises in 2021 by the Fire Brigades Union: <https://redplaque.org.uk/plaque/colin-townsley>, accessed 16 January 2023.

[89] *The Guardian*, 18 November 2017, <https://www.theguardian.com/uk-news/2017/nov/18/kings-cross-fire-victims-honoured-30-years-on>.

been redeveloped, and the surrounding areas gentrified and regenerated, few who remember these fires remain in the local area and there is unlikely to be little interest among homeowners or renters (least of all landlords) to be reminded of the horrific experiences that took place in their homes. Most fires in HMOs have therefore long been forgotten, only occasionally to be brought up as a reminder of the invisibility and expendability of marginal communities. When I was writing a blog post on the fortieth anniversary of the Kilburn fire in early 2020, I was struck by how quickly the victims were stripped of their identities and reduced to simplistic, incorrect and insulting descriptions (as 'elderly women', 'destitute women' and 'inadequate alcoholics'). Doing so renders these women – and the many other victims of the fires discussed here – as unimportant. It removes them from their individual lives. Ultimately, it allows those institutions who have failed them to avoid feelings of guilt towards them. The 'great unswept corner of housing policy' was yet another reminder of the human costs of deregulation and the failure of an inhumane state to care for those who most needed our care.

Conclusion

The need to learn *before* and *after* Grenfell

This book has traced the development of a regulatory approach towards fire safety and building control across twentieth-century Britain and its subsequent diminution from the late 1970s to the present day. It has shown how deregulation, both as ideology and practice, was dominant in shaping policymaking in these realms for successive governments since 1979. Predominantly concerned with relaxing and removing existing controls over the market, restricting the state's powers of inspection, certification and enforcement, and devolving responsibility for safety to the individual, deregulation resulted in a confusing regulatory landscape under which it was legal to permit flammable and combustible cladding to be placed on tall buildings in which many millions of individuals and families lived. Historicising deregulation and multiple-fatality fires over the long twentieth century thus sheds light on the longer-term historical context to the 2017 disaster at Grenfell Tower, which has been largely peripheral to the public inquiry. While the fire has been shown to be the result of particular local circumstances, specific to the North Kensington community, it also reflects a historical moment defined by a confluence of national and international factors, not least neoliberalism, deregulation, globalisation and austerity.

While the official proceedings reveal undoubted systemic failures in governance and organisational management, the inquiry into the Grenfell fire has also exposed an ingrained culture of institutional insouciance towards public safety, especially in protecting those most vulnerable to fire risks. Institutional indifference permeates central and local government as well as the construction industry, and is manifested in a 'race to the bottom' of safety standards, commercial greed, local authority cost-cutting and the belittling attitudes of a political elite that resists calls for a more precautionary approach to fire safety because of its likely impact on 'UK plc'. It is also reflected in the testimony of individual politicians and senior civil servants during the inquiry: in one particularly egregious moment, a former secretary of state incorrectly paid tribute to the 'nameless 96 victims' of the fire, confusing the fire with the 1989 Hillsborough stadium disaster. Such an example illustrates a casual nonchalance and has been bravely challenged by those with 'lived experience' of the fire and the public inquiry; in this case, the local community, survivor groups and bereaved families.[1]

Such an insouciant attitude has revealed the inability of governments, as well as other stakeholder organisations, to learn and change from their historic encounters with failure. It is further manifested in the unwillingness of senior ministers and industry leaders to accept responsibility for failure immediately following a catastrophic event: rather, the inquiry's lead counsel has criticised 'a merry-go-round of buck passing' from responsible persons across the private and public sectors.[2] Thus, lasting systemic change cannot be expected until this historic culture of indifference and 'buck passing' is conceded and challenged from within; that is, by those who have up to now been complicit in its continued operation. As Gill Kernick, a fire safety consultant and one-time resident of Grenfell Tower, has argued, what is required is a 'democratisation of change' in which a greater diversity of communities are invited to disrupt the status quo and brought into the fold in order to hold governments to account for their policies as they affect everyday lives.[3] This final chapter will therefore draw two broad conclusions about how a history that foregrounds its 'public purpose' can help policymakers and other responsible organisations challenge the institutional culture that created the conditions under which the fire occurred.

Firstly, history shows us that a cultural change is required at the heart of government, especially one that embraces the value of regulation for public safety and the wellbeing of the nation. For too long, deregulation has been regarded by politicians, industry leaders and the right-wing media as the solution to Britain's social and economic malaise, largely due to an entrenched belief that the market needs to be freed of all restrictions and can effectively become its own regulator. Yet the reality is quite the opposite and history reveals a need to question such deeply held contextual assumptions. The seventy-two victims of the Grenfell fire, as well as the many hundreds of other lives lost in the forgotten disasters examined in this book, tragically and repeatedly underline the marketplace's inability to protect vulnerable communities, as well as central government's unwillingness to step in and impose appropriate controls or sanctions. What is required, argue Hilary Cooper and Simon Szreter in their compelling history of the Covid-19

[1] GTI, Closing submission by Sam Stein QC on behalf of the bereaved, survivors and residents, 10 December 2018, 193–4; Hackitt, *Final Report*, 5; Apps, *Show Me the Bodies*, 306–7.

[2] GTI, Opening statement by counsel to the inquiry, Richard Millett QC, 27 January 2020, 18.

[3] Kernick, *Catastrophe*, 221–5.

pandemic, is a new mindset within central government that embraces 'collectivist individualism', reinforces the 'psychological contract' between the state and its citizens and stops seeing regulation as an unnecessary burden – on businesses, people and the state. The wellbeing of a nation can be assessed by how far a state is prepared to go to protect the most vulnerable people who fall under its duty of care. Indeed, universal protections coupled with a commitment to public safety are a positive means of enhancing the personal freedoms of the whole of society while also offering tangible benefits to the economy through a healthy and productive workforce.[4]

There is historical precedent here. Britain's post-war governments recognised the terrible costs that fire damage was causing to the nation and its productive wellbeing, and prioritised public safety and security as core values that underpinned the building of the welfare state. So too did industry leaders. Matched funding from the government and the fire protection industry was fundamental in improving the safety of building materials, processes and products that fuelled the country's reconstruction as well as the consequent boom in consumer spending. That drive to govern using research-informed and evidence-based policy underpinned the growth and diversification of the economy, but this has been lost through successive decades of untrammelled deregulation, privatisation and abandonment of state controls. Our economic and political leaders have lost sight of the benefits of a well-regulated country, not least in terms of the tangible benefits that regulatory governance can bring to our collective health and prosperity as a nation.

Secondly, in order to re-embrace the value of regulatory governance as being in the best interests of society, there is a need for a new arrangement of checks and balances that simplifies, as well as strengthens, the existing patchwork system. Tentative steps were made with the 2021 Fire Safety Act and the following year's Building Safety Act, not least with greater clarification issued for the role of 'responsible persons' for multi-occupied residential buildings. Further piecemeal change is on the horizon with the announcement, in December 2022, that government is consulting on requiring second staircases in new tall residential buildings, mandating sprinklers in all new care homes to help firefighters with building evacuations and adopting tougher European fire testing requirements.[5] However, more could still be done to bring about, in the words of the Department for

---

[4] Cooper and Szreter, *After the Virus*, 251–85; Kernick, *Catastrophe*, 222–3.

[5] Department for Levelling Up, Housing and Communities, 'Government Proposes Second Staircases to Make Buildings Safer', 23 December 2022, <https://www.gov.uk/government/news/government-proposes-second-staircases-to-make-buildings-safer>.

Levelling Up, Housing and Communities' legal counsel during his final statement at the Grenfell Inquiry, 'lasting changes to overhaul a regulatory system that has been shown to have been unfit for purpose'.[6] In this sense, politicians and senior civil servants need to act bravely, embracing a greater diversity of voices from those with lived experiences on new regulatory bodies that monitor, enforce and hold to account the decisions made in their interest. Those who have lived in unsafe buildings, lost friends, relatives or neighbours in fires, and entered burning buildings to save lives should be listened to by those who are tasked with creating a new regulatory system that is fit for purpose. Public safety should be realigned as the priority of everyone in a post-Grenfell era; joint regulation, with a fuller diversity of lived experience and knowledge, would help ensure that the system of checks and balances is in place to make this happen in practice.

Again, history reveals a precedent for joint regulatory working in the form of the Joint Fire Research Organisation (JFRO) and the Central Fire Brigades Advisory Council (CFBAC), both of which drew together experts to lead on fire safety research and advise on national policy in the decades following the end of the Second World War. JFRO's fire and building research stations – later amalgamated into the Building Research Establishment (BRE) – conducted world-leading research into fire behaviour and made a material contribution to improved safety in the home as well as the workplace, especially between the late 1940s and 1970s. CFBAC, on the other hand, brought together a coalition of ranks and experiences from across the fire service to advise government on national policy, including the representative unions of frontline firefighters as well as senior fire officers. Taking BRE back under national ownership, as advocated by the London mayor, Sadiq Khan, and the Fire Brigades Union, would signal a decisive step in the move to make public safety a national priority by establishing a new statutory body to advise the government on fire service matters.[7] Were ministers also to reconstitute BRE's membership, with representatives drawn from the fire and rescue service as well as consumer and residents' bodies who speak on behalf of local communities, alongside more traditional voices representing the engineering and building professions, this would signal systemic change by focusing regulatory attention on building safety

---

[6] GTI, Closing Statement by Jason Beer, King's Counsel, 10 November 2022, 25.

[7] See Tweet by Tom Copley, London Deputy Mayor for Housing, @tomcopley, 29 December 2022, <https://twitter.com/tomcopley/status/1608483554253574144>, accessed 3 January 2023; Fire Brigades Union, 'FBU Calls for Grenfell Building Safety Body to Be Nationalised', 13 May 2022, <https://www.fbu.org.uk/news/2022/05/13/fbu-calls-grenfell-building-safety-body-be-nationalised>.

beyond the design and completion stages. It would also hopefully end the 'path of least intervention' approach taken by governments, which, as we have seen here, only leads to more deaths and misery for families and communities.

Learning from disasters requires a fuller range and diversity of voices and experiences to be heard than is currently allowed. Learning must also by necessity involve listening to uncomfortable truths, especially if government is to be compelled to act in the moral as well as the economic interests of the nation. Citizen participation extends beyond the public inquiry process – not least because this formal process of learning often happens *after* the event – and should be embedded within the formal mechanisms that produce and monitor existing regulations. A more inclusive, honest and historically reflective approach towards building regulation – in which governments learn and publicise the lessons from past fires *before* future ones occur – would herald lasting change, including greater security for communities. This would be the most fitting memorial to those who lost their lives in past building fires.

Bibliography

Manuscript collections

Eastside Community Heritage
- 2018_esch_RoPo_04, Interview transcript between James King and Sam Webb, 20 March 2019.
- 2019_esch_RoPo_03, Interview transcript between James King and Frances Clarke, 8 March 2019.

London Metropolitan Archives
- GLC/AR/ENG/SE/1/1-9, Ronan Point inquiry papers, technical studies, correspondence and press cuttings.

Modern Records Centre, University of Warwick
- MSS.346/4, Fire Brigades Union policy and administration papers, campaigns and reports of annual conference.
- MSS.346/81-119 and MSS.346/4/239/6-33, *The Firefighter*, <https://wdc.contentdm.oclc.org/digital/collection/fbu>, accessed 7 March 2023.

Newham Borough Archives, Stratford Public Library
- 363.5 Newham Tower Block Tenants Campaign: leaflets and ephemera.
- 728 Ronan Point: miscellaneous news cuttings.
- VF/NEW/728 Housing: miscellaneous news cuttings.

Royal Borough of Kensington and Chelsea Archives
- [unreferenced] Lancaster West Estate: site plans and correspondence, 1970–1.
- [unreferenced] folder of misc. newspaper cuttings from 1975.
- Acc/2001/002/Box 14: council planning documents.
- Acc/2001/003/Box 24: Notes for tenants, newsletters and miscellaneous ephemera.

The National Archives, Kew
- AT/49, AT/66, AY/21, CAB/129, DSIR/4, DSIR/36, HLG/51, HLG/52, HLG/117-118, HLG/157, HO/45, HO/346, HO/363, MH/154, MH/160, WORK/75.

Parliamentary papers and other official publications[1]

Annual reports of Her Majesty's Chief Inspector of Fire Services since 1947.

---

[1] Please note that all published legislation was accessed either via UK Parliamentary Papers or the UK government website, <https://www.legislation.gov.uk>. Hansard debates

Annual reports of the Building Research Establishment, 1972–97.

Annual reports of the Department of Scientific and Industrial Research, 1947–64.

Annual reports of the Department of the Environment, 1990–7.

Annual reports of the Joint Fire Prevention Organisation's Fire Research Board, 1945–71.

Sir George Bain, *The Future of the Fire Service: Reducing Risk, Saving Lives* (London: Office of the Deputy Prime Minister, 2002).

Building Regulations Advisory Committee, *First Report*, Cmd. 2279 (London: HMSO, 1964).

Cabinet Office, *Better Accounting for the Taxpayer's Money: The Government's Proposals*, Cmd. 2929 (London: HMSO, 1995).

Cabinet Office, *One-in, One-Out: Statement of New Regulation* (London: HMSO, 2011).

Department for Business, Energy and Industrial Strategy, *Reforming the Framework for Better Regulation: Summary of Responses to the Consultation* (London: HMSO, 2022).

Department for Communities and Local Government, *The Building Regulations 2000. Fire Safety. Approved Document B. Volume 2 – Buildings Other Than Dwellinghouses* (London: NBS, 2006).

Department of the Environment, *White Paper on the Future of Building Control in England and Wales*, Cmd. 8179 (London: HMSO, 1981).

Department of the Environment, *The Building Regulations: Mandatory Rules for Means of Escape in Case of Fire* (London: HMSO, 1985).

Department of the Environment, *The Building Regulations 1985: Approved Document B – Fire Spread* (London: HMSO, 1985). See also *The Building Regulations: Approved Document B – Fire Safety*, 1992, 2000, 2002, 2006, 2007, 2010, 2013, 2019, 2020 and 2022 editions.

Department of the Environment, *The Building Regulations 1985: Manual to the Building Regulations 1985* (London: HMSO, 1985).

were accessed from UK Parliamentary Papers. All remaining published papers were accessed via the British Library.

Department of the Environment, *Consultation Paper on Houses in Multiple Occupation* (London: HMSO, 1988).

Department of the Environment, *Houses in Multiple Occupation: Guidance to Local Housing Authorities on Standards of Fitness under Section 352 of the Housing Act 1985* (London: HMSO, 1992).

Department of the Environment, *Houses in Multiple Occupation: Consultation Paper on the Case for Licensing* (London: HMSO, 1994).

Department of the Environment, *Improving Standards in Houses in Multiple Occupation* (London: HMSO, 1995).

Department of the Environment and Fire Offices' Committee, *United Kingdom Fire Statistics* (London: HMSO, 1972–80).

Department of the Environment, Home Office and Welsh Office, *Guide to Means of Escape and Related Fire Safety Measures in Certain Existing Houses in Multiple Occupation* (London: HMSO, 1988).

Department of the Environment, Trade and the Regions, *Licensing of Houses in Multiple Occupation – England: A Consultation Paper* (London: HMSO, 1999).

Department of Trade and Industry, *Burdens on Business: Report of a Scrutiny of Administrative and Legal Requirements* (London: HMSO, 1985).

Department of Trade and Industry, *Competitiveness: Forging Ahead*, Cmd. 2867 (London: HMSO, 1995).

Edmundson, P.R. and Hubbard, G.I., *A Review of the Fire Precautions Act 1971* (London: Home Office, 1993).

Fennell, D., *Investigation into the King's Cross Underground Fire*, Cmd. 499 (London: Department of Transport, 1988).

Griffiths, H., *Report of the Inquiry into the Collapse of Flats at Ronan Point, Canning Town* (London: HMSO, 1968).

Hackitt, J., *Building a Safer Future: Independent Review of Building Regulations and Fire Safety – Interim Report*, Cmd. 9951 (London: HMSO, 2017).

Hackitt, J., *Building a Safer Future: Independent Review of Building Regulations and Fire Safety – Final Report*, Cmd. 9607 (London: HMSO, 2018).

Home Office, *Guide to the Fire Precautions Act 1971. 1 Hotels and Boarding Houses* (London: HMSO, 1972).

Home Office, *Future Fire Policy: A Consultative Document* (London: HMSO, 1980).

Home Office, *Fire Statistics United Kingdom* (London: HMSO, 1981–88).

Home Office, *A Review of the Fire Precautions Act 1971: A Consultative Document* (London: HMSO, 1985).

Home Office, *Fire Safety Legislation for the Future: A Consultation Document* (London: HMSO, 1997).

Home Office, *Personal Emergency Evacuation Plans in High-Rise Residential Buildings – Recommendations from the Grenfell Tower Inquiry Phase 1 Report: Government Response* (London: HMSO, 2022).

Joint Committee of the Building Research Board, *Fire Grading of Buildings Part I: General Principles and Structural Precautions* (London: HMSO, 1946).

Joint Fire Research Organisation, *Effects of Draughts on the Burning of Portable Oil Heaters* (London: HMSO, 1960).

Jupp, K., *Report of the Committee of Inquiry into the Fire at Fairfield Home, Edwalton, Nottinghamshire, on 15 December 1974*, Cmd. 6149 (London: HMSO, 1975).

Minister without Portfolio, *Lifting the Burden*, Cmd. 9571 (London: HMSO, 1985).

Ministry of Housing and Local Government, *Model Bye-Laws, Series IV: Buildings* (London: HMSO, 1952).

Moore-Bick, M., *Grenfell Tower Inquiry: Phase 1 Report – Volume 1* (London: HMSO, 2019).

Moore-Bick, M., *Grenfell Tower Inquiry: Phase 1 Report Overview* (London: HMSO, 2019).

Morgan, P., Jones, D. and Clinch, S., *Summary of Fires Investigated: April 1991 to March 1992* (London: HMSO, 1992).

Office of the Deputy Prime Minister, *Our Fire and Rescue Service*, Cmd. 5808 (London: HMSO, 2003).

Popplewell, O., *Committee of Inquiry into Crowd Safety and Control at Sports Grounds: Interim Report*, Cmd. 9585 (London: HMSO, 1985).

Rogowski, F.W., Ramaprasad, R. and Southern, J.R., *Fire Performance of External Thermal Insulation for Walls of Multi-Storey Buildings* (Watford:

Building Research Establishment, 1988). See also 2nd edition (2003) and 3rd edition (by Colwell, S. and Baker, T., 2013).

Thomas, A. and Hedges, A., *The 1985 Physical and Social Survey of Houses in Multiple Occupation in England and Wales* (London: HMSO, 1986).

Vowden, D., *Report of the Committee of Inquiry into the Fire at Coldharbour Hospital, Sherborne on 5 July 1972*, Cmd. 5170 (London: HMSO, 1972).

Wilson, H., 'Labour's Plan for Science', 1 October 1963, <http://nottspolitics .org/wp-content/uploads/2013/06/Labours-Plan-for-science.pdf>.

Other contemporary published reports

Association of District Councils, *The Challenges of Multiple Occupancy: A Fresh Look at HMOs* (London: ADC, 1988).

Binney, V., Harkell, G. and Nixon, J., *Leaving Violent Men: A Study of Refuges and Housing for Battered Women* (London: Women's Aid Federation, 1982).

British Standard Definitions for Fire Resistance, Incombustibility, and Noninflammability of Building Materials and Structures, Including Methods of Test, No. 476 (London: British Standards Institution, 1932).

British Standard Code of Practice CP 3: Chapter IV: Precautions against Fire. Part 1: Flats and Maisonettes (London: British Standards Institution, 1971, 1978 editions).

Building Research Establishment, *Large Panel Systems: The Structure of Ronan Point and Other Taylor Woodrow – Anglian Buildings* (Watford: BRE, 1985).

Building Research Establishment, *Housing Defects Reference Manual* (London: E & FN Spon, 1991).

Cameron, D., Conservative Party conference speech, 5 October 2011, <https:// www.bbc.co.uk/news/uk-politics-15189614>.

Campaign for Bedsit Rights, *Bedsit Rights: A Handbook for People Who Live in Bedsits* (London: CHAR, 1989).

Campaign for the Homeless and Roofless, *CHAR Report 1981/92* (London: CHAR, 1982).

Cantlie, J.D., *Report of the Summerland Fire Commission* (Isle of Man: Government Office, 1974).

Clingan, G.P., 'National building regulations', *Journal of the Royal Society of Arts*, 93:4688 (1945), pp. 205–14.

Critchley, R., *Fire Safety Guide* (London: Campaign for Bedsit Rights, 1991).

Elder, J., *Guide to the Building Regulations 1985* (London: Butterworth Architecture, 1986).

Fire Brigades Union, *Who Will Pick Up the Pieces? FBU Response to the Government's Interdepartmental Review of Fire Safety Legislation and Enforcement* (Kingston upon Thames: FBU, 1994).

Fire Brigades Union, *The Grenfell Tower Fire: A Fire Caused by Profit and Deregulation* (Kingston upon Thames: FBU, 2019).

Harrison, P., *Inside the Inner City: Life under the Cutting Edge* (London: Penguin, 1983).

Holiday Which?, *Fire in Hotels: An Investigation* (London: Consumers' Association, 1979).

Hotel and Catering Industry Board, *Act Quickly! Seconds Count!* (London: Hotel and Catering Industry Board, 1984).

Kirkham, F., Assistant Deputy Coroner, Inner Southern District of Greater London, to the Secretary of State for Communities and Local Government, Eric Pickles, 'Lakanal House Fire 3 July 2009', 28 March 2013.

Mitchell, G.E., *Model Building Byelaws Illustrated*, 2nd edition (London: B.T. Batsford, 1947).

National Consumer Council, *Deathtrap Housing: Tacking Fire Hazards for Tenants of Houses in Multiple Occupation* (London: NCC, 1991).

Raynsford, N., *Substance Not Spin: An Insider's View of Success and Failure in Government* (Bristol: Policy Press, 2016).

Read, R.E.H., 'Fire Risks in High-Rise Buildings', *Building Research Establishment Information Paper* (1979).

Report of the Tribunal of Inquiry on the Fire at the Stardust, Artane, Dublin on the 14th February, 1981 (Dublin: Stationery Office, 1982).

Seabright, D., *Fire and Care: An Enquiry into Fire Precautions in Residential Homes* (London: Personal Social Services Council, 1979).

Taylor, J. and Cooke, G., eds., *The Fire Precautions Act in Practice* (London: Architectural Press, 1978).

Watson, S. and Austerberry, H., *Housing and Homelessness: A Feminist Perspective* (London: Routledge, 1986).

Webb, S., *Annual Spot Safety Survey* (London: National Tower Blocks Network, 1990).

Wright, W.S. and Powell-Smith, V., *The Building Regulations Explained and Illustrated for Residential Buildings* (London: Crosby Lockwood & Son, 1967, 1972 and 1978 editions).

News sources

- *BBC News*
- *Bedsit Briefing*
- *Bedsit Rights*
- *BRE News*
- *Building*
- *Camden New Journal*
- *Chartered Municipal Engineer*
- *Construction News*
- *Daily Express*
- *Daily Mail*
- *Daily Mirror*
- *Daily Telegraph*
- *Evening Standard*
- *Financial Times*
- *Fire*
- *Firefighter*
- *Fire Prevention*
- *Fire Protection Association Journal*
- *Fire Research Notes*
- *Inside Housing*
- *Journal of the Royal Society of Arts*
- *Kensington News & Post*
- *Liverpool Daily Post*
- *Liverpool Echo*
- *Liverpool Evening Express*
- *New Civil Engineer*
- *Newham News*
- *Newham Recorder*
- *Private Eye*
- *RICS Building Control Journal*
- *Roof*
- *The Builder*
- *The Guardian*

- *The Municipal Journal*
- *The Spectator*
- *The Standard*
- *The Surveyor*
- *The Times*
- *The View*
- *Willesden and Brent Chronicle*

Websites

Disability Rights UK: <https://www.disabilityrightsuk.org>.

Fire Brigades Union: <https://www.fbu.org.uk>.

Fire Safety Science Digital Archive: <https://publications.iafss.org/public ations/frn/info>.

Grenfell Tower Inquiry, proceedings and evidence: <http://www.grenfell towerinquiry.org.uk>.

Grenfell United: <https://grenfellunited.org.uk>.

HM Government: <https://www.gov.uk>.

Labour Party manifestos: <http://www.labour-party.org.uk/manifestos>.

London Fire Brigade: <https://www.london-fire.gov.uk>.

Margaret Thatcher Foundation: <https://www.margaretthatcher.org>.

Royal Institution of Chartered Surveyors: <https://www.rics.org/uk>.

Secondary sources

Abrams, L., Kearns, A., Hazley, B. and Wright, V., *Glasgow: High-Rise Homes, Estates and Communities in the Post-War Period* (London: Taylor & Francis, 2020).

Almond, P. and Esbester, M., *Health and Safety in Contemporary Britain: Society, Legitimacy, and Change since 1960* (Basingstoke: Palgrave Macmillan, 2019).

Andresen, K. and Müller, S., eds., *Contesting Deregulation: Debates, Practices and Developments in the West since the 1970s* (New York: Berghahn Books, 2017).

Andrews, A., 'Truth, justice, and expertise in 1980s Britain: the cultural politics of the New Cross Massacre', *History Workshop Journal*, 91:1 (2021), pp. 182–209.

Apps, P., *Show Me the Bodies: How We Let Grenfell Happen* (London: Oneworld Publications, 2022).

Apps, P., Barratt, L. and Barnes, S., 'The paper trail: the failure of Building Regulations', *Inside Housing*, 23 March 2018.

Beaumont, C., *Housewives and Citizens: Domesticity and the Women's Movement in England, 1928–64* (Manchester: Manchester University Press, 2013).

Bhandar, B., 'Organised state abandonment: the meaning of Grenfell', *The Sociological Review Blog*, 19 September 2018.

Bingham, A. and Conboy, M., *Tabloid Century: The Popular Press in Britain, 1896 to the Present* (Oxford: Peter Lang, 2015).

Black, L., Pemberton, H. and Thane, P., eds., *Reassessing 1970s Britain* (Manchester: Manchester University Press, 2013).

Booth, P., *Thatcher: The Myth of Deregulation*, IEA Discussion Paper No. 60 (London: Institute of Economic Affairs, 2015).

Boughton, J. *Municipal Dreams: The Rise and Fall of Council Housing* (London: Verso, 2019).

Bowley, M., *Innovations in Building Materials: An Economic Study* (London: Gerald Duckworth, 1960).

Bradley, K., *Lawyers for the Poor: Legal Advice, Voluntary Action and Citizenship in England, 1890–1990* (Manchester: Manchester University Press, 2019).

Briganti, C. and Mezei, K., eds., *Living with Strangers: Bedsits and Boarding Houses in Modern English Life, Literature and Film* (London: Bloomsbury, 2018).

Brooke, S., 'Living in "new times": historicizing 1980s Britain', *History Compass*, 12:1 (2014), pp. 20–32.

Bulley, D., Edkins, J. and El-Enany, N., eds., *After Grenfell: Violence, Resistance and Response* (London: Pluto Press, 2019).

Canter, D., ed., *Fires and Human Behaviour*, 2nd edition (London: Fulton, 1990).

Cartwright, A., 'Rented worlds: bedsits, boarding houses and multiple occupancy homes in postwar London, 1945–1963', University of London PhD, 2020.

Cartwright, A., 'The un-ideal home: fire safety, visual culture and the LCC (1958–63)', *The London Journal*, 46:1 (2021), pp. 66–91.

Clarke, S., 'Pure science with a practical aim: the meanings of fundamental research in Britain, circa 1916–1950', *Isis*, 101:2 (2010), pp. 285–311.

Clifton, J., Lanthier, P. and Schröter, H., 'Regulating and deregulating the public utilities 1830–2010', *Business History*, 53:5 (2011), pp. 659–72.

Cooper, H. and Szreter, S., *After the Virus: Lessons from the Past for a Better Future* (Cambridge: Cambridge University Press, 2021).

Cornish, F., '"Grenfell changes everything?" Activism beyond hope and despair', *Critical Public Health*, 31:3 (2021), pp. 293–305.

Courtney, R., 'Building Research Establishment – past, present and future', *Building Research & Information*, 25:5 (1997), pp. 285–91.

Cowan, D., ed., *Housing: Participation and Exclusion* (London: Routledge, 1998).

Crook, T. and Esbester, M., eds., *Governing Risks in Modern Britain: Danger, Safety and Accidents c. 1800–2000* (London: Palgrave Macmillan, 2016).

Crowson, N.J., 'Introduction: the voluntary sector in 1980s Britain', *Contemporary British History*, 25:4 (2011), pp. 491–8.

Crowson, N.J., 'Revisiting the 1977 Housing (Homeless Persons) Act: Westminster, Whitehall, and the homelessness lobby', *Twentieth Century British History*, 24:3 (2012), pp. 424–47.

Crowson, N.J., Hilton, M., McKay, J. and Marway, H., 'Witness seminar: the voluntary sector in 1980s Britain', *Contemporary British History*, 25:4 (2011), pp. 499–519.

Davies, A., '"Right to Buy": the development of a Conservative housing policy, 1945–1980', *Contemporary British History*, 27:4 (2013), pp. 421–44.

Davies, A., Jackson, B. and Sutcliffe-Braithwaite, F., eds., *The Neoliberal Age? Britain since the 1970s* (London: University of College London Press, 2021).

Davies, W., 'Neoliberalism: a bibliographic review', *Theory, Culture & Society*, 1:7–8 (2014), pp. 309–17.

Delap, L., Szreter, S. and Holland, F., 'History as a resource for the future: building civil service skills', *History & Policy*, 17 March 2015.

Drach, A. and Cassis, Y., eds., *Financial Deregulation: A Historical Perspective* (Oxford: Oxford University Press, 2021).

Drysdale, D. and Watts, J., 'David Rasbash and the Department of Fire Engineering', *Fire Safety Science News*, 35 (2013), pp. 14–15.

Dunleavy, P., *The Politics of Mass Housing in Britain, 1945–1975: A Study of Corporate Power and Professional Influence in the Welfare State* (Oxford: Clarendon Press, 1981).

Easthope, L., *When the Dust Settles: Stories of Love, Loss and Hope from an Expert in Disaster* (London: Hodder & Stoughton, 2022).

Edgerton, D., *The Rise and Fall of the British Nation: A Twentieth-Century History* (London: Penguin, 2019).

Ewen, S., *Fighting Fires: Creating the British Fire Service, c.1800–1978* (Basingstoke: Palgrave, 2010).

Ewen, S., 'Socio-technological disasters and engineering expertise in Victorian Britain: the Holmfirth and Sheffield floods of 1852 and 1864', *Journal of Historical Geography*, 46 (2014), pp. 13–25.

Ewen, S., 'The tragedy of the hidden homeless – living in death-trap hostels in Thatcher's Britain', *Fire Brigades Union Blog*, 18 March 2020, <https://www.fbu.org.uk/blog/tragedy-hidden-homeless-living-death-trap-hostels-thatchers-britain>.

Ewen, S. and Andrews, A., 'The media, affect, and community in a decade of disasters: reporting the 1985 Bradford City stadium fire', *Contemporary British History*, 35:2 (2021), pp. 25–83.

Finlayson, A., *Making Sense of New Labour* (London: Lawrence & Wishart, 2003).

Firth, P., *Four Minutes to Hell: The Story of the Bradford City Fire* (Manchester: Parrs Wood Press, 2005).

Flanagan, K., Clarke, S., Agar, J., Edgerton, D. and Craig, C., *Lessons from the History of UK Science Policy* (London: British Academy, 2019).

Francis, M., '"A crusade to enfranchise the many": Thatcherism and the property-owning democracy', *Twentieth Century British History*, 23:2 (2012), pp. 275–97.

Gaskell, S.M., *Building Control: National Legislation and the Introduction of Local Bye-Laws in Victorian England* (London: Bedford Square Press, 1983).

Gerstle, G., *The Rise and Fall of the Neoliberal Order: America and the World in the Free Market Era* (Oxford: Oxford University Press, 2022).

Glendinning, M. and Muthesius, S., *Tower Block: Modern Public Housing in England, Scotland, Wales and Northern Ireland* (New Haven, CT: Yale University Press, 1994).

Glew, H., *Gender, Rhetoric and Regulation: Women's Work in the Civil Service and the London County Council, 1900–55* (Manchester: Manchester University Press, 2016).

Gorse, C. and Sturges, J., 'Not what anyone wanted: observations on regulations, standards, quality and experience in the wake of Grenfell', *Construction Research and Innovation*, 8:3 (2017), pp. 72–5.

Green, A.R., *History, Policy and Public Purpose: Historians and Historical Thinking in Government* (Basingstoke: Palgrave Macmillan, 2016).

Green, J., 'Anglo-American development, the Euromarkets, and the deeper origins of neoliberal deregulation', *Review of International Studies*, 42 (2016), pp. 425–49.

Hanley, L., *Estates: An Intimate History* (London: Granta Books, 2012).

Harper, R., *Victorian Building Regulations* (London: Mansell, 1985).

Hazley, B., Abrams, L., Kearns, A. and Wright, V., 'Place, memory and the British high rise experience: negotiating social change on the Wyndford Estate, 1962–2015', *Contemporary British History*, 35:1 (2021), pp. 72–99.

Hilton, M., 'The death of a consumer society', *Transactions of the Royal Historical Society*, 18 (2008), pp. 211–36.

Hilton, M. and McKay, J., eds., *The Ages of Voluntarism: How We Got to the Big Society* (Oxford: Oxford University Press, 2011).

Hilton, M., McKay, J., Crowson, N.J. and Mouhot, J.-F., *The Politics of Expertise: How NGOs Shaped Modern Britain* (Oxford: Oxford University Press, 2013).

Hodkinson, S., *Safe as Houses: Private Greed, Political Negligence and Housing Policy after Grenfell* (Manchester: Manchester University Press, 2019).

Hodkinson, S. and Murphy, P., 'The fire risks of purpose-built blocks of flats: an exploration of official fire incident data in England: interim research findings', July 2021, <https://www.bafsa.org.uk/wp-content /uploads/bsk-pdf-manager/2021/07/Fire-Risks-of-Purpose-Built-Blocks -of-Flats-An-exploration-of-Official-Fire-Incident-Data-in-England .pdf>, accessed 7 March 2023.

Holmes, C., *A New Vision for Housing* (London: Routledge, 2006).

Hong, N.S. and Rowley, C., 'Globalization and Hong Kong's labour market: the deregulation paradox', *Asia Pacific Business Review*, 6:3–4 (2000), pp. 174–92.

Hull, A., 'War of words: the public science of the British scientific community and the origins of the Department of Scientific and Industrial Research, 1914–16', *British Journal for the History of Science*, 32:4 (1999), pp. 461–81.

Jackson, B. and Saunders, R., eds., *Making Thatcher's Britain* (Cambridge: Cambridge University Press, 2012).

Johnson, P. and Lane, B., 'In memoriam: Professor Margaret Law', *Fire Technology*, 53 (2017), pp. 2041–3.

Kay, J. and Vickers, J., 'Regulatory reform in Britain', *Economic Policy*, 3:7 (1988), pp. 285–351.

Kernick, G., *Catastrophe and Systemic Change: Learning from the Grenfell Tower Fire and Other Disasters* (London: London Publishing Partnership, 2021).

Knowles, C.C. and Pitt, P.H., *The History of Building Regulation in London 1189–1972* (London: Architectural Press, 1972).

Knowles, S.G., 'Learning from disaster? The history of technology and the future of disaster research', *Technology and Culture*, 55:4 (2014), pp. 773–84.

Lambert, R., 'Central and local relations in mid-Victorian England: the Local Government Act Office, 1858–71', *Victorian Studies*, 6:2 (1962), pp. 121–50.

Ledger, R.M., 'A transition from here to there?' Neo-liberal thought and Thatcherism', Queen Mary University PhD thesis, 2014.

Ledger, R.M., *Power and Political Economy from Thatcher to Blair: The Great Enemy of Democracy?* (London: Routledge, 2021).

Leggett, D. and Sleigh, C., eds., *Scientific Governance in Britain, 1914–79* (Manchester: Manchester University Press, 2016).

Lewis, J., 'New Labour's approach to the voluntary sector: independence and the meaning of partnership', *Social Policy & Society*, 4:2 (2005), pp. 121–31.

Ley, A.J., 'Building control: its development and application 1840–1936', Open University MPhil, 1990.

Ley, A.J., *A History of Building Control in England and Wales 1840–1990* (Coventry: RICS Books, 2000).

Leys, C., *Market-Driven Politics: Neoliberal Democracy and the Public Interest* (London: Verso, 2001).

Macdonagh, O.J.M., 'The nineteenth-century revolution in government: a reappraisal', *Historical Journal*, 1:1 (1958), pp. 52–67.

MacLeod, R., ed., *Government and Expertise: Specialists, Administrators and Professionals, 1860–1919* (Cambridge: Cambridge University Press, 1988).

Majone, G., 'Paradoxes of privatization and deregulation', *Journal of European Public Policy*, 1:1 (1994), pp. 53–69.

Mäkhä, R., 'Basil Fawlty as a "pre-Thatcherite" conservative in Fawlty Towers', *Journal of European Popular Culture*, 8:2 (2017), pp. 109–23.

Malpass, P., ed., *The Housing Crisis* (London: Croom Helm, 1986).

Malpass, P. and Murie, A., *Housing Policy and Practice*, 5th edition (London: Macmillan, 1999).

Melville, H., *The Department of Industrial and Scientific Research* (London: George Allen and Unwin, 1962).

Moore, S., Wright, T. and Taylor, P., *Fighting Fire: One Hundred Years of the Fire Brigades Union* (Oxford: New Internationalist, 2018).

Moran, M. *The British Regulatory State: High Modernism and Hyper-Inflation* (Oxford: Oxford University Press, 2007).

Morgan, K. and Morgan, J., *Portrait of a Progressive: The Political Career of Christopher, Viscount Addison* (New York: Oxford University Press, 1980).

Nixon, R., *Slow Violence and the Environmentalism of the Poor* (Cambridge, MA: Harvard University Press, 2011).

Nixon, S., 'Life in the kitchen: television advertising, the housewife and domestic modernity in Britain, 1955–1969', *Contemporary British History*, 31:1 (2017), pp. 69–90.

O'Hagan, A., 'The tower', *London Review of Books*, 7 June 2018.

Ortolano, G., *Thatcher's Progress: From Social Democracy to Market Liberalism through an English New Town* (Cambridge: Cambridge University Press, 2019).

Pellew, J., 'The Home Office and the Explosives Act of 1875', *Victorian Studies*, 18:2 (1974), pp. 175–94.

Phillips, I., 'The Summerland fire disaster' (2020), available at <https://www.summerlandfiredisaster.co.uk>, accessed 7 March 2023.

Phillips, S. and Martin, J., *Grenfell and Construction Industry Reform: A Guide for the Construction Professional* (London: Routledge, 2022).

Preston, J., *Grenfell Tower: Preparedness, Race and Disaster Capitalism* (Basingstoke: Palgrave, 2019).

Prosser, T. and Taylor, M., *The Grenfell Tower Fire: Benign Neglect and the Road to an Avoidable Tragedy* (Shoreham-by-Sea: Pavilion Publishing, 2020).

Rhodes, G., *Inspectorates in British Government: Law Enforcement and Standards of Efficiency* (London: Allen and Unwin, 1981).

Robinson, E., Schofield, C., Sutcliffe-Braithwaite, F. and Thomlinson, N., 'Telling stories about post-war Britain: popular individualism and the "crisis" of the 1970s', *Twentieth Century British History*, 28:2 (2017), pp. 268–304.

Saint, A., *Towards a Social Architecture: The Role of School Building in Post-War England* (New Haven, CT: Yale University Press, 1987).

Saumarez Smith, O., 'The lost world of the British leisure centre', *History Workshop Journal*, 88 (2019), pp. 180–203.

Scott, P., 'Friends in high places: government-industry relations in public sector house-building during Britain's tower block era', *Business History*, 62:4 (2020), pp. 545–65.

Shapely, P., 'Tenants arise! Consumerism, tenants and the challenge to council authority in Manchester, 1968–92', *Social History*, 31:1 (2006), pp. 60–78.

Shildrick, T., 'Lessons from Grenfell: poverty propaganda, stigma and class power', *The Sociological Review Monographs*, 66:4 (2018), pp. 783–98.

Simon, B., *The Hamlet Fire: A Tragic Story of Cheap Food, Cheap Government, and Cheap Lives* (London: The New Press, 2017).

Sirrs, C., 'Health and safety in the British regulatory state, 1961–2001: the HSC, HSE and the management of occupational risk', London School of Hygiene & Tropical Medicine PhD, 2016.

Smith, H., 'The Ronan Point scandal, 1968–1993', University of Cambridge MPhil, 2020.

Stedman Jones, D., *Masters of the Universe: Hayek, Friedman, and the Birth of Neoliberal Politics* (Princeton, NJ: Princeton University Press, 2014).

Sutcliffe-Braithwaite, F., 'Neo-liberalism and morality in the making of Thatcherite social policy', *Historical Journal*, 55:2 (2012), pp. 497–520.

Tombs, S., *Social Protection after the Crisis: Regulation without Enforcement* (Bristol: Policy Press, 2017).

Tomlinson, J., *The Politics of Decline: Understanding Post-War Britain* (London: Routledge, 2001).

Tosh, J., *Why History Matters* (Basingstoke: Palgrave Macmillan, 2008).

Vernon, J., 'Heathrow and the making of neoliberal Britain', *Past & Present*, 252 (2021), pp. 213–47.

Walton, J., *The Blackpool Landlady: A Social History* (Manchester: Manchester University Press, 1978).

Wetherell, S., 'Freedom planned: enterprise zones and urban non-planning in post-war Britain', *Twentieth-Century British History*, 27:2 (2016), pp. 266–89.

Wetherell, S., *Foundations: How the Built Environment Made Twentieth-Century Britain* (Princeton, NJ: Princeton University Press, 2020).

Williamson, A., *Conservative Economic Policymaking and the Birth of Thatcherism, 1964–1979* (New York: Palgrave, 2015).

Woods, A., *A Manufactured Plague: The History of Foot-and-Mouth Disease in Britain* (London: Routledge, 2004).

Index

professional periodicals, 17–18
  Caterer and Housekeeper, 45
  Fire, 43
  Inside Housing, 7
  Municipal Journal, 32
  Roof, 85
  Surveyor, The, 95
  *Surveyor and Municipal and County
    Engineer*, 17
public health, 8, 21–4
public inquiries, 4–5, 14, 48–9, 53,
  107–8. *See also* Grenfell Tower
  Inquiry
race, racism, 93, 97. *See also* housing in
  multiple occupancy (HMOs); rental
  property market
Rachman, Peter, landlord, 92
Rasbash, David, fire engineer, 68
Raynsford, Nick, MP, Minister of State
  for Local and Regional Government
  (2001–5), 55–6
Read, R.E.H., fire engineer, 61–2
red tape, 9, 19, 29–30, 34, 52, 54
  Red Tape Challenge, 41
regulation
  better regulation, 54, 103
  costs of, 11–12, 37, 46, 49–50, 56
  criticisms of regulations, 20, 41, 49,
    54, 109
  hyper-innovative, 51–2
  micro-practices of, 40–41, 58–9,
    85
  path of least intervention, 20, 88,
    92, 101–2, 110–11
  regulate to deregulate, 13–14, 34,
    41–2, 53
  regulatory state, 51–2, 54–5
  value of regulation, 108–11
  See also building regulations;
    deregulation; fire precautions;
    self-regulation

rental property market
  deregulation of, 100–104
  racial inequalities of, 96–7
residents
  experience of fire, 1, 80–82
  neglect of concerns, 1, 80, 87, 93, 108
  safety campaigns and mobilisation,
    2–3, 75, 80–82, 97, 100
Rhys-Williams, Brandon, MP, 95
risk, risk assessment, 8, 101. *See also* fire
  precautions
Robens, Lord, politician, trade unionist
  and civil servant, 29
Ronan Point Tower-Block Disaster
  (1968), 3–4, 26, 67, 72–3, 79, 81–2, 92
Royston Hill, Glasgow, 80
Rushdie, Salman, novelist, 97
St Pancras New Church, 105
safety. *See* building safety; fire safety;
  residents
safety inspectorates, 20
sanitary control, 22
scalds, scalding, 75
scientific governance, 62–3, 72–5
  and civil service, 63, 67–9
  self-governance, 75–84
Second World War, 17–18, 23–4, 66
self-regulation, 8, 13, 29, 30–3, 49, 53–4,
  103. *See also* deregulation; regulation
Sharples, Richard, MP, Minister of
  State at the Home Office (1970–2),
  44
slow disaster, 6
slums, slumlords, 92, 94, 97, 101
Smith, Harry, H.M. Chief Inspector of
  Fire Services, 44
social democracy, 31
Southampton, Hampshire, 99
space heaters, 3, 68, 73–5, 98
stay put, 5, 14, 24, 38, 67, 79–80. *See
  also* compartmentation; firefighters

Printed in the USA
CPSIA information can be obtained
at www.ICGtesting.com
CBHW051549070824
12743CB00010B/55